A *Lillenas* DRAMA RESOURCE
HOW-TO BOOK

PRODUCING
and
DIRECTING

Drama for the Church

by
Robert M. Rucker

Lillenas PUBLISHING COMPANY

KANSAS CITY, MO 64141

Cover design by Crandall Vail
Cover photo by Rick Day
Costume plates by Terry Beckham
Technical plates by Karen Rine

Portions of the introduction contain excerpts from *Create a Drama Ministry*, by Paul M. Miller and Dan Dunlop, © 1984 by Lillenas Publishing Company. "Aims in Lighting" and "First Steps in Lighting Design" reprinted with permission of Routledge, Inc., Publishers, from *The Stage Lighting Handbook*, Third Edition, © 1987 by Francis Reid. "Doing Straight Makeup" and "Character Makeup" reprinted with permission of Clark Publishing from *Basic Drama Projects*, Fifth Edition, © 1987 by Fran Averett Tanner. "Glossary of Stage Terms" from *The Complete Play Production Handbook*, by Carl Allensworth and Dorothy Allensworth. Copyright © 1981 by Carl Allensworth. Reprinted by permission of HarperCollins Publishers.

Unless otherwise indicated, all Scripture quotations in this book are from the *Holy Bible, New International Version*® (NIV®). Copyright © 1973, 1978, 1984 by International Bible Society. Used by permission of Zondervan Publishing House. All rights reserved.

PRODUCING and DIRECTING
Drama for the Church

To Dad and Mom, who bring to life the proverb "Parents are the pride of their children."

To my wife, Amy, whose support and love enriches my life beyond measure.

And to all the hardworking, self-sacrificing drama ministries like Mustard Seed and First Drama Ensemble, for whom this book is written.

Contents

Foreword   9
Preface   11
Acknowledgments   13
Introduction   15

PART I: **PREPARATION**   23
    1. Approaching the Process   25
    2. Scheduling Rehearsals and The Stage Manager   41
    3. Conducting Auditions   51

PART II: **FROM WORDS TO PICTURES**   61
    4. Analyzing the Playscript   63
    5. Designing the Stage Composition   74
    6. The Relationship of Dialogue to Movement   94

PART III: **ACTORS AND ACTING**   103
    7. Basic Ingredients in Acting Techniques   105
    8. Working with the Actor's Voice   110
    9. Characterization   117
    10. Pathology of Bad Acting   123

PART IV: **TECHNICAL PRODUCTION**   129
    11. Constructing the Set Design   131
    12. Lighting the Action   142
    13. Costuming the Actors   160
    14. Makeup   179

Notes   193
Glossary of Stage Terms   195
Selected Bibliography for Directors   205

Foreword

It was one of the early Lillenas Drama Conferences, held each February in Greater Kansas City, when an earnest young man came up to me and asked if I needed help. I suspect I was acting frantic and he was taking pity on me. I assured him that everything was under control. A few weeks later I received a letter and some program suggestions from him. Probably more to pacify him than to help me, I contacted him, which in turn began a process that evolved into Rob Rucker's irreplaceable contribution to the organization and programming of our annual conclave.

Rucker's seminars and workshops on all phases of drama ministry are always Standing Room Only. His emphasis on ministry and proclamation provide a much-needed rationale for church drama and is the heart of a work-in-progress monograph on the theology of theatre.

Producing and Directing Drama in the Church is a landmark publication. While others have released production how-to books in a variety of formats, Robert Rucker has given the church world a thorough text that not only provides the church drama director with the details and reasons-why but also gives the school administrator and classroom teacher a textbook for Christian theatre classes.

Robert Rucker has been a drama director in schools and churches for over 15 years and has studied drama at the Juilliard School Theatre Center in New York. He holds graduate degrees in music, education, and theology from the Ohio State University, Dallas Seminary, and Southern Methodist University. He is a choral conductor, conference speaker, lecturer, teacher at the graduate level, and continues to direct and add to more than 700 performances in theatre and entertainment.

Robert and his wife, Amy, make their home in Dallas.

PAUL M. MILLER
Lillenas Drama Resources

Preface

Religious drama in Western civilization has traveled an uneven path. In the 20th century, Christian drama groups grew through the first quarter of the century, but most were terminated during the Great Depression. In the 1950s, theatre arts practiced by Christians gained significant momentum, especially in Catholic and Protestant universities, colleges, and some churches. But by the 1970s this advancement began slowing. Perhaps television and radio technologies supplanted our esteem of live theatre. It seems as though Christian drama is winding down to a mere novel communication for occasional church events. On the other hand, some churches are using drama for evangelism and hiring full-time drama ministers to administrate the program.

Five hundred years ago, the Church virtually abandoned the theatre to merchant guilds who caricatured theological themes and exaggerated our degenerate whims for entertainment. Theatre left the hands of the theists and has yet to return. This book is assembled with the hope that contemporary Christian theatre will regain the prevalence it once had. If triteness can be replaced by excellence, perhaps we may attract Christian artists to help us open our minds to the power of the dramatic arts. While the path of salvation is narrow, the means of expression is broad.

This book is designed to address the need for increasing professionalism among teachers of theatre arts in the local church and college. Although some churches currently enjoy the work of professionally trained theatre arts leaders, many others retain only the desire for a theatre arts program, lacking the essentials of time, talent, and money. Some harbor the archaic attitude that theatre is only secular street burlesque. These obstacles may be significantly diminished by an adept coordination of directorial and acting training. This book should contribute to the local church drama ministry and help fill the need for theologically and artistically trained actors/directors of Christian theatre arts.

Part I outlines the necessary preparation every director undertakes to mount a theatrical production, with an overview of the whole process in chapter one. Scheduling rehearsals, as well as a brief section on one of the most important members of the team, the stage manager, are discussed in chapter two. Auditions and casting complete the first section of the director's preparation. Part II begins with the script analysis process, the basis from which most of your directorial decisions will be made. From your analysis, you can begin applying the techniques used to transform the words of the script into a living picture, covered in chapters five and six. Part III includes four chapters introducing the basic ingredients in acting techniques and characterization, closing with a list of common indications of less than polished acting. Finally, Part IV contains fours chapters covering the fundamental considerations of technical production: including sets, lights, costumes, and makeup, respectively.

Producing and Directing Drama for the Church is intended to be a starting point for the beginning or intermediate drama director who wishes to pursue excellence in the arts. It is not an exhaustive resource by any means. The acting chapters provide only an overview of the craft of acting, written as an orientation for a director, not for actors. The very basic concepts of composition and picturization form "pigments" for the director's palate from which application can be made. But space does not permit the inclusion of the infinite ways innumerable scenes may be directed. Directing is best learned by doing, and doing it often. The information in this book points directors in the right direction, but each director must travel the path with his or her own choices and decisions. When finished with the reading of this book, the director is encouraged to study numerous other professional theatre publications. In the mean time, dig in and enjoy!

Acknowledgments

I wish to acknowledge the following musicians, actors, directors, dancers, writers, pastors, artists, and technicians who have had a significant role in shaping my thinking on this subject and continue to champion excellence in the arts ministry: Debbie Clegg, Robert Petty, Buff and Dulcey Delcamp, James Gallagher, Deborah Craig-Claar, Paul McCusker, Larry Haron, Elizabeth Sarles, Thomas Groves, Mike Edwards, Reg Grant, Robin Smith, Neil Lines, Ed Pierce, Rodger Williams, Thomas Cragoe, Craig Schilling, Jeannie Hellman, Don Regier, Ionia Zalenka, Barbara Brinson, Linda Tomczak, Neil Curran, Bill Bryan, and Roger Deschner (whom I deeply miss).

I also wish to thank Karen Rine, who made this project look marvelous by transforming concepts into pictures, and for doing it so well and asking so little in return.

Last, but definitely not least, I thank Paul Miller, our drama minister-at-large, for providing vision, taking risks, and persevering with the gifted team at Lillenas, on behalf of all Christian artists who genuinely desire to serve our Lord.

Introduction

A wonderful new energy continues breathing throughout the Christian Church these days. It's really not new; it's been around to some degree ever since Christ said, "You will be my witnesses" (Acts 1:8). This breath of fresh air is the recognition that ministry need no longer be considered the responsibility of a special class of professionals. Neither can ministry be hemmed in by pulpits and stained-glassed attitudes. Ministry is being recognized for what it is—service. People-saturated service. Ministry is invading the long suspected art of drama. It is helping return a secular art form to its original state—the church. For too many years we have allowed the world to take a highly influential means of communication and squeeze it into a mold that has had a negative influence on society. After all, creativity is an attribute of God.

The first revealed act of God in recorded history is His act of creating, ex nihilo (out of nothing). We are creatures in His image, and we reflect His image by our own works of creation. Our creative works,

How Creativity Manifests the Image of God

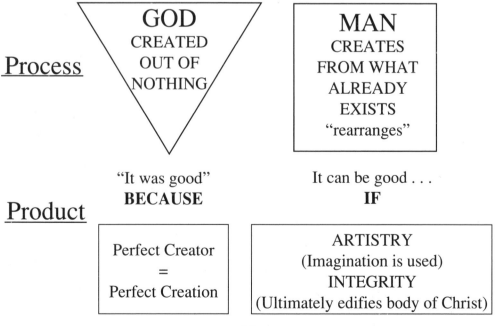

however, are not ex nihilo. Humankind engages in *creation continua,* which is the ongoing, sustaining activity of creating from that which has already been created. It is appropriate then that our words *creative* and *creativity* indicate an infinite process of discovering and rearranging existing elements. God's creation was perfect. Our creativity is not. We must judge our creativity by our use of our imagination. Does it **edify** (Philippians 4:8; Galatians 5:22)? And is it committed to **excellence**?

Critics have been heard raising the observation that the proclamation or message, which ought to be central in church drama, is too often lost in the theatrical trappings. The play and its performance becomes the end in itself. Granted, that may be a liability, but it is just as possible in any other ministry to get caught up in methods and materials. This must be kept in check but is no reason to throw it out and disqualify the pursuit of excellence in art that is Christian. Skeptics say there is no justification for arts in ministry and we should only be concerned with saving a lost world. Yes, we should be concerned with saving a lost world. But God gave us a degree of one of His attributes: creativity.

Creativity justifies the existence of artistic thoughts and impulses. Art resides as an abstract form within creative humanity. It waits to be realized and actualized into a concrete form. This creative power bestowed upon men and women enables humanity to draw upon the beauty that exists in music, poetry, and the visual and performing arts. By giving art meaning and relevance, Christians become stewards of grace and beauty in a world of disorder and relativism. There is no need to justify the arts or Christians in the arts. As one author so simply puts it:

> Art does not need justification, nobody has to be excused for making art. Artists do not need justification, just as . . . taxi drivers, police officers or nurses do not need to justify with clever arguments why they are doing their work . . . The meaning of the job is in the love for God and neighbor . . . Art itself is a potential given by God. We human beings only discover this and use it in a better or poorer way. This truth also makes it impossible to make a kind of religion out of art as is often the case with modern art . . . art can have a place in religious worship.[1]

If, then, art is a natural component of creation, and the image of God (imago Dei) is reflected in human's creativity, why do artistic pursuits remain foreign to many evangelical church programs? We distrust secular theatre artists. We lack education and experience in religious theatre arts. We have seen too many church skits lacking subtlety and nuance, failing to be thought-provoking, or poorly executed. Ultimately, we fail to exercise consistently our imagination, a primary source for humankind's creativity and ability to reflect God's attributes. Another author observes:

> We have an amazing, intricate, incredibly imaginative God to have invented us and our world. We have an amazingly unselfish God, as well. How many of us would have imparted to our creatures so much of our own essence, our imagination? We see the results in music, painting, dance, paint, fiction and non-fiction, in the craft arts as well as the fine arts . . . We ignore God's work with the excuse that we are spending our time getting to know Him directly through prayer, Bible study, and so forth. These should not be ignored. But what about all the rest? We could no more know a chef by ignoring his food than we can know God by ignoring His creation. We need an insatiable curiosity to know, and we don't have it. Knowledge feeds the imagination, which will translate into worship.[2]

Indeed, it cannot be disputed that worship is the heart of a rationale for theatre arts ministries within the paradigms of the local church.

Drama (from the Greek *dromenon*, "to do") refers to several things. It is the whole body of literature written for the theatre. It applies to any conflict or contrast of characters intended to be presented on a stage. It is the art of writing and producing plays. It is action, a series of events having vivid and striking interest.[3]

The Definition of

D R A M A

from the Greek word *dromenon* meaning "to do"

- the body of literature written for the theatre

- conflict of characters to be presented on stage

- art of writing and producing plays

- action, events having vivid or striking interest

Remembering our Lord at the Communion table, the ceremony of marriage, and the act of baptism are events of vivid and striking drama. Old Testament Hebrews, with their temple worship services, employed drama and pantomimed salvation with symbolic objects (2 Chronicles 5).

Ancient worship was not just pantomime. The public reading of Scripture enabled people to value and receive instruction from the recitation of the spoken Word (Deuteronomy 5). The Passover events are fraught with drama and symbolism (Exodus 12).

The Books of Ruth, Esther, and Job are exemplary of dramatic literature. Many scholars believe the Bible is the "the great code" from which all world literature is patterned.[4]

The prophets used drama to depict the future or to teach a vital lesson. One prophet acted a role before Ahab to expose the king's disobedience (1 Kings 20:35-43). Isaiah was instructed to walk partially naked and barefoot for three years because Assyria would defeat Egypt and Ethiopia, nations to which Judah displaced their trust from God (Isaiah 20). Jeremiah placed a yoke on his neck symbolizing God's use of Nebuchadnezzar as an instrument of judgment (Nehemiah 27—28). Ezekiel was instructed by God to build replicas of cities to be used as dramatic symbols. He also split hairs from his own head and laid on one side of his body for extended periods of time to teach God's people pointed lessons (Ezekiel 4—5). Ahijah tore his clothing into 12 pieces (1 Kings 11), and Zedekiah made for himself a set of horns symbolizing the defeat of the Syrians (1 Kings 22). Ezra led a group of 15 Levites in a choral reading of the Law (Nehemiah 9:15). Agabus portrayed a scene of capture to show Paul that he would be captured if he went to Jerusalem (Acts 21:10).

The New Testament illustrates that when we could not comprehend God, the Word became flesh, and the incarnation of Christ Jesus portrayed God before us. Jesus, as the perfect storyteller, related eternal, spiritual truths via the structure of parables. These parables are supreme examples of dramatic irony. Dramatic irony involves a remark made for two audiences, one of which will hear and not understand, the other of which will hear and understand, not only the remark but also the first hearer's incomprehension.

One of the more concise opening lines in dramatic literature is, "There was a man who had two sons" (Luke 15:11). Immediately the hearer is caught up in a story that leads him directly to the heart of truth in a way that a more polemic technique could never do.

Without question, the passion of our Lord is the ultimate dramatic event on the timetables of history. With divine insight, Jesus led His disciples in a seeming dress rehearsal of an event that would transpire in a matter of hours. Central to Jesus' teaching ministry was the use of commonplace elements—bread, wine, wind, fish, grain—in which everyday items became symbols of redemption and eternity.

Drama has long been an ingredient of Christian worship. For hundreds of years priests and worshipers have played out the richly symbolic ritual of the mass. In vaulted naves and candle-lit chancels, worship had traditionally contained a dramatic element: "the Word enacted." Long before most people were able to read the Bible for themselves, English worship adopted simple pantomime embellishments for Easter and Christmas services.

By the 10th century the clergy expanded the liturgical drama into a series of short plays that illustrated the main events in the Christian calendar. As these homespun performances grew in complexity, audience enthusiasm and the lack of proper decorum necessitated relocating the plays from church sanctuaries to outdoor stages. At the same time the clergy-actors relinquished their involvement to lay performers.

As the laity assumed artistic management of church drama, the miracle plays came into being. The purpose of these works was to provide vivid reality to the essential Christian doctrines. With supplements from the Old Testament and church history, the plays ranged in subject matter from the fall of Lucifer to the Day of Judgment. A unique feature of these performances was the pageant wagon upon which the plays were performed. These portable stages were, as their name indicates, wagons that could be hauled from village to village, insuring that everyone had an opportunity to see and hear the great truths from the Bible dramatized.

By the 1500s the secular influence of the Renaissance had thoroughly permeated English drama. No longer were biblical history, doctrine, and life's noble virtues the basis for dramatic presentation. Troupes of professional actors took over the work from amateur performers. The influence of professionalism, demands of the royal family, and the growing spirit of humanism necessitated a change to entertainment with more socially accepted secular themes, primarily illicit love, political intrigue, and satirical jibes at the church.

During the latter part of that century, and into the 1600s, the most recognized playwright of all time—William Shakespeare—produced his tragedies, comedies, and historical chronicles. It was during this time that James I, king of England, commissioned that translation of what is now commonly known as the King James Version of the Bible.

Through the 18th, 19th, and now the 20th century, drama continued to be an influential purveyor of ideas as well as entertainment. The roots of revolution and promotion of political ideology can be traced to the theatre of every century. This power cannot be understated. The millions affected by television, motion pictures, and the so-called legitimate stage are testimonials to the potential power of the dramatic media. If society as a whole and its individuals can be so affected by a couple of hours of playacting, why not provide the church with this same medium but sanctified by the use of plays and entertainment for the fellowship of His people and to His glory? Why not affect hearts and lives with drama that reflects eternal values?

Religious drama is capable of taking all of these elements of good storytelling, and then adds another dimension: the capacity of captivating an audience and asking them to identify so strongly with the situation that every viewer is compelled to transfer what he hears and sees on the stage to his own life. Herein lies a major similarity between secular theatre and drama that is Christian; but the ends are not the same. Christian drama uses the strong identification factor as a means for allowing the spirit of God to convince and convict. As with Jesus' parables, church drama has the ability to take spiritual truth and couch it in an appealing narrative to which every person in the audience can respond. This is the staring point in implementing drama as a ministry.

Because of its mandate for an enlivened imagination, drama is a vital and effective communication tool in Christian education. Competing with a media-saturated world in which secular entertainment voraciously gratifies the souls of the lost, the church counters by using Christian drama as a means for allowing the Holy Spirit to move men and women to the truth. Drama is one of several powerful mediums for the teaching of biblical material and the examination of the dynamics of the Christian life.

The drama ministry of the church provides a solid foundation for fellowship because of its format for participation and service, involving the whole person and opening the door for discussion and service. A drama ministry in the church is as natural as Jesus telling parables to communicate spiritual concepts. A drama ministry can be engaging because it has an innate capacity for immediacy (presented "live"). As a teaching vehicle for self-discovery, drama carries tremendous impact when participants relate spiritual concepts to everyday life.

Ministry is a way of facilitating people to make use of their talent in a way that will bring glory to God and maturity to the participant. When ministry and drama are coupled, the results provide an outlet for the use of one's God given gifts, and a provision is made for the proclamation of the gospel in a way that will attract attention.

The ministry concept of drama has a direct influence upon those who participate. It provides service opportunities for those with skills that the church has not always used. In a typical play production there are tasks that demand the skills of directors, actors, designers, technicians, electricians, carpenters, seamstresses, administrators, comptrollers, and so on. Few ministries in the program of the church unify such a diversity of gifts toward a common purpose.

Furthermore, the apostle Paul's words, "I have become all things to all men so that by all possible means I might save some" (1 Corinthians 9:22), form an appropriate starting point in any discussion of unique opportunities to proclaim Christ. The "all means" must include many appropriate media, that is, proclamation of life in Christ by the preached word, music, teaching, films, video, storytelling, and drama. The list may be unending, but each medium has the potential of being a viable method of proclamation. Of these methods, drama may have one of the greatest potentials for the church's ministries of outreach:

- Drama incorporates methodology that Jesus used: storytelling, object lessons, and audience involvement. Drama is natural.
- Drama has origins in the church; it is time for the church to redeem the medium. Drama is historical.
- Drama has the innate capacity of immediacy; it attracts attention and involves the audience. Drama is engaging.
- Drama relates spiritual concepts to everyday life in nonthreatening terms. Drama is relevant.
- Drama opens the door to further discussion, activity, and unity. Drama is stimulating.

A drama ministry affords expanded opportunities for worship and praise, teaching and nurture, participation, fellowship, and evangelism. What more can be said to validate the essential importance of a drama ministry in your church?

PART I

PREPARATION

►►► ONE ◄◄◄

Approaching
the Process

Starting with a thorough understanding of the overall directorial process helps guide you to your final goal: public presentation. Every director progresses through the same basic stages. Each play, every group of actors, and various technical demands require unique scheduling structures. But a logical order of the many-faceted meetings, deadlines, and rehearsals unifies many elements into a manageable whole. What seems like an unconquerable nemesis for the volunteer church drama director (who usually has a full-time occupation besides, be it motherhood or else) becomes a series of attainable short-term projects. The goal is to produce an experience from which the congregation can learn something and enjoy it.

The first step in approaching a drama production is to understand each phase of the process: studying and theorizing, strategizing, bringing to life, and fusion. Within each phase includes responsibilities organized into a series of goals. If you allow a general outline to guide you through the production step by step, unnecessary distractions or premature, hasty decisions can be minimized. Like many processes, some steps interrelate with another, overlapping at times or necessarily occurring earlier than anticipated. Nevertheless, a prudent director understands the comprehensive operation of a dramatic or musical production.

Months before any auditions are announced, a period of studying and theorizing ignites the imagination of the director preparing for a dramatic event. Selecting the play requires weighing, evaluating, examining, and reflecting on options that relate to the spiritual dynamics of your specific congregation. Researching the final selection brings you to the essential meaning of the playwright's words and the eventual effects the production will have on its audience. These effects on the audience are the final results of the author's, director's, and designer's conception of the play. Fashioning each step of the process to achieve the desired end provides plenty of creativity for everyone involved.

The second period is one of strategizing and brings forth the nuts and bolts of the play production. Once a play has been selected, delineate the available funds to the respective material needs. Firm up the schedule of every rehearsal and every deadline, however slight. Select qualified and talented people to assume various responsibilities. Ideally, you will be able to enlist the creative powers of a scenic designer or an architect or some other willing persons to design the sets, costumes, and props. Finally, post an announcement of auditions and cast the play.

After the cast has been assembled, the third period is bringing to life characters from actors and action from dialogue. Directing and acting training merge into one process as the play begins to take shape. While the actors are rehearsing, the carpenters are building the sets and the designers are giving life to costumes and props.

Finally, all of the diverse elements merge into the final period of fusion. Technical and dress rehearsals display the efforts of actors, designers, directors, and crew on the stage. Three of the final five rehearsals are considered technical rehearsals, and the final two rehearsals before the play opens are the dress rehearsals. It may seem as though the work is done when the curtain rises, but some drama ministries require administrative tasks during performance runs and tours. An outline of the process may be listed as follows:

Phase One: Studying and Theorizing	Play Selection
	Analysis
	Envisioning
Phase Two: Strategizing	Staffing
	Budgeting
	Scheduling
	Designing
	Casting
Phase Three: Bring to Life	Rehearsals
	Construction
Phase Four: Fusion	Technical Rehearsals
	Dress Rehearsals
	Final Presentation
	Strike

While a little practical experience and common knowledge can guide most people through several steps of the process, such as auditions and scheduling, other steps will be dealt with in a more detailed manner.

PHASE ONE: STUDYING AND THEORIZING

The first phase is a time when you should experience the greatest freedom in your creative thinking; endless possibilities for play selection may be entertained and evaluated. Should you do a musical? Will it be about an Old Testament character? A New Testament character? A topical musical? A staged oratorio? A contemporary composition? Should we compose our own 45-minute drama with a small cast or do a one-man monologue of 2 Timothy in modern dress? What about an evangelistic play for outreach dinner drama? Or should you do liturgical drama suitable for worship services? Is it time to expand the ongoing drama ministries into all of these areas?

Play Selection

Play selection has a major effect on determining the quality of a production. A well-written play is not reason enough for its selection. It must be appropriate for the audience, commensurate with the available talent, modifiable to the auditorium or facility in which it will be presented, and sustainable by the budget prepared for it.

The first consideration in play selection may be the **spiritual dynamics** of your audience. Guide your options toward modern dress plays written by contemporary playwrights who are in touch with current life-styles if family health is to be your theme. Perhaps your fellowship would appreciate an Old Testament theme in connection with a series on Old Testament characters. Unlike professional directors who choose plays for a variety of occupational and artistic reasons, the evangelical director makes his choice based primarily upon the relevancy of a dramatic work to the spiritual maturity of the fellowship.

The second consideration of utmost importance is the artistic **integrity of the playscript**. The play must be intelligently conceived and constructed, exhibiting the marks of an artistic playwright. The materials of dialogue, settings, conflict, characterization, dramatic irony, etc., should withstand literary scrutiny by evidencing nuance, subtlety, harmony, and balance. Larger fellowships having extensive drama ministries may make selections based on concurrent themes for services or goals for the season.

Third, consider the **content** of the play. Is it theologically accurate? Does it respect the theological traditions precious to your fellowship? Does it have the potential to inspire worship? Can it be powerful enough to change an audience member's view of life? Productions of plays or musicals that fail to evidence an attempt to challenge the lives of the audience is nothing more than entertainment. Although entertainment is healthy in a believer's life and may play a significant role in many of your endeavors, an ongoing drama ministry ultimately seeks to alter the heart attitudes of those who participate in and attend the play. If a play or musical does not motivate an audience or cast member to contemplate what they have seen on the stage, perhaps the content is lacking. Remember, one of your goals is to serve others by helping them draw closer to their Lord and Master Jesus Christ.

Fourth, consider your **resources** of space, talent, and money. Most religious drama groups prepare and present their works not on theatre stages but in any available space with any available talent and money. Consequently, you should consider plays that will be well served by existing resources within your fellowship. Bigger is not necessarily better. Regarding money, a play can be produced for as little as the cost of the script or for as much as your imagination and budget will allow. Some plays may require special effects beyond your financial capabilities. If your artistic imagination cannot surmount these obstacles, perhaps it would be better to select another play.

As a final note to play selection, it should be mentioned that brainstorming will be a profitable activity. Freedom characterizes the period of studying and theorizing. Exert no limits on yourself in the early periods of play selection. Read as many plays as you can and obtain as much new material as is available to you. Jot down your responses in the margins of plays as you read them. Shelve your favorites together so that you may return to them later. Consider acquiring rights to adapt nondramatic material such as novels or biographies. Solicit opinions from qualified people concerning your speculations and final choices. Create a team of readers whose sole purpose is to uncover new scripts from the church at large. Collaborate with a gifted writer from within your fellowship in the creation of new plays. Most of all, enjoy thi- time of discovery.

Analysis

While a more detailed section on script analysis will be discussed later, the director should become an expert on the play. Research forms the breadth of knowledge you bring to each rehearsal and uncovers unlimited ideas for the artistic aims in play production.

Research involves outlining the script into manageable sections, identifying the high points, the structural elements of the dramatic action, and anticipating the demands of the production. How many sets are there? What is the size of the cast? What are the demands for costumes? Where do the climaxes occur? How intense is the "rising action"? What is the syntax of each speech and why? How are the figures of speech and allusions used? Many of these questions will be discussed later.

Seek outside sources for your research. It is not uncommon for authors of plays to be living in the United States or England. Seek the author's own remarks about the play: What did he have in mind while writing the play? What are his impressions of other productions? What does the play communicate to other people? What have other directors said about the play? Can you get a video of another production?

Continue to read textbooks and periodicals concerning every facet of the theatre. Energetic and thorough research is the first step toward excellence. A fine director does not "wing it." Every play and every scene should be thought through carefully and creatively, with the intention of advancing the effectiveness and philosophy of the team.

Envisioning

From the completed research you can begin to describe and explain what the play is about, how it will look, the interpretation of the text, the design of the settings, how it will be staged, edits and additions to the script, casting considerations, acting training, and the overall look of the play in performance. You may not be able to mark precisely where the phase of research ends and the envisioning begins. Envisioning as a result of research may guide you to further research, and during rehearsals (well after the studying and theorizing period has ended) newly discovered concepts may warrant additional research.

Begin developing a hypothetical cast list from the available talent. Outline general approaches you may want to take toward rehearsals, how you will train the actors to achieve desired results. If you do not have the time, talent, and money to implement a comprehensive actor training program, determine which ingredients of acting training you will include in the rehearsal period.

During this stage, prepare your script by transforming it into a director's notebook. This is a registry of your ideas conceived in your research. Extensive notes may be recorded in the margins of the script by pasting it onto an 8½" x 11" format. Cut or unbind the pages of two scripts. Tape or paste each page of the script onto each side of the pa-

Constructing a Promptbook/Production Notebook

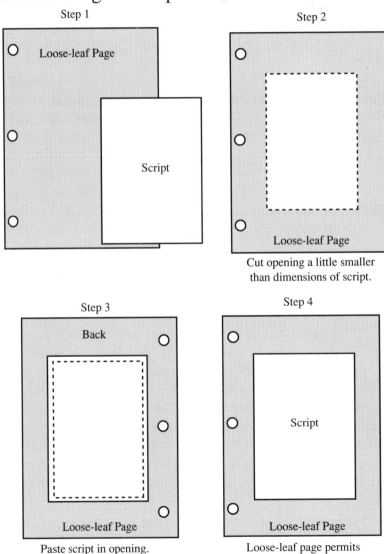

Step 1

Loose-leaf Page

Script

Step 2

Loose-leaf Page

Cut opening a little smaller
than dimensions of script.

Step 3

Back

Loose-leaf Page

Paste script in opening.

Step 4

Script

Loose-leaf Page

Loose-leaf page permits
marginal notes and cues.

per, allowing room around the script for notes. Record all cuts and additions in your notebook. This is not to be confused with the stage manager's promptbook, which will be a record of actor movement and production-related cues and information, commonly called the production notebook.

PHASE TWO: STRATEGIZING

As you move into the strategizing stages, assemble other talented people to flesh out the conclusions born in the studying and theorizing phase. In this phase you will staff the production, design the set and technical support, and budget expenses.

Staffing

To achieve a more thorough approach to planning, it is recommended that you staff the production. Pray for and call together a group of cooperative and talented people who will comprise the production staff, consisting of the following:

Director	In addition to blocking the scenes of the play, oversees the entire production.
Stage Manager/ Assistant Director	Coordinates activities of all participants, supervises budgetary concerns, promotional activities, publicity, and tickets.
Scenic Designer/ Technical Director	Supervises the physical production and coordination of technical elements by designing the scenic picture and stage properties.
Musical Director/ Conductor	In the event of a musical, supervises all of the music.
Choreographer	Responsible for all dancing and movement of musical production numbers.

While the above staff members represent the essential elements of your staffing needs, you may be able to add any or all of the following:

Costume Designer	Responsible for the designing and constructing and renting of all the costumes.
Wardrobe Mistress	Supervises the assignment of costumes to actors and maintains the integrity of each costume and the costume collection at large.
Properties Master	Supervises the creation of the properties list and the assembling, alterations, and organization of all stage properties.

Makeup Coordinator	Designs and executes the stage makeup.
Assistant Musical Director	Assists with the rehearsals for the chorus and individual instruction with principals in a musical production.
Assistant Choreographer	Helps with the chorus of dancers and provides individual instruction when necessary.
Lighting Designer	Assumes the responsibility of lighting the show should the scenic designer choose not to do so.
Publicist	Assumes responsibility for promotion of the performances, programs, and management of the auditorium (house).
Budget Coordinator	Oversees the formation of the production budget; maintains records of all financial activities.

Possible Organizational Flow Chart

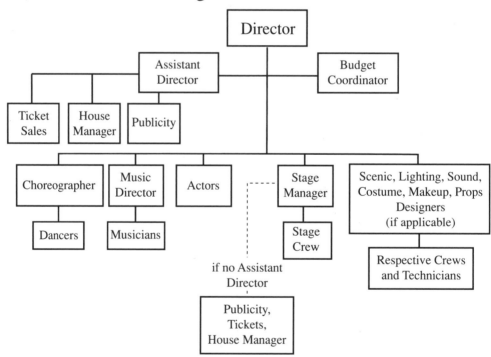

In the absence of professionally oriented theatre personnel in your fellowship, be creative in your selection of staff. A carpenter may make a good technical director or an architect an excellent scene designer. Highly organized housewives make superb stage managers. High school students active in their drama departments may lend invaluable assistance. An illustrator may serve as a scene painter. Ask a graphic artist to create logos for publicity and promotion. Many times you will find less qualified but exceptionally willing individuals who will give it their best shot. Together, you can build a dedicated production staff under your gentle and professional leadership.

Assemble your staff for the first meeting. Present the structure of the play in the form of a production plan. This is a simple outline that gives a concise and quick overview of the entire production. Display the material of the play in chart form with a column for scene divisions, including the setting, time, and season of each scene, and musical numbers when applicable. Another column should include a description of the scenery for each scene, another column for lighting, another for the description of people in the scene, another for the description of their costumes, and the last column a description of the method of changing from one scene to another. During this meeting, forge through the data until everyone understands the presented course of action.

Now discuss the production schedule. Begin with the performance dates and work back. As a team, agree upon deadlines for each area of the production. It has been the experience of the author to schedule deadlines unrealistically premature so as to thwart procrastination and the tragic delays of unfinished production tasks, which set the whole project behind. In every situation, deadlines are agreed upon by all involved. Promote delegation among the staff. The more people you can get involved in your ministry, greater is the opportunity for the Holy Spirit to use the production in others' lives. Oftentimes the greatest spiritual activity of a play impacts the hearts of the participants. Encourage all activities to be completed at approximately the same time so that the various elements can come together. Otherwise, one group may be disadvantaged while waiting on the completion of an essential element of the final presentation. If everyone understands what has been agreed upon, the anticipation of accomplishment may be enhanced and accountability among the production staff is encouraged. If production staff members need financial resources to achieve their goals, it will be necessary to prepare a budget.

Example of Production Plan

Reinhardt Players
WHERE HE LIES
A One-act Play in Four Scenes
by Lawrence G. Enscoe
Technical Director: __Karen Rine__

SCENE	SETTING	SCENERY	LIGHTING	CHARACTERS	COSTUMES	SCENE CHANGE METHOD
One	present, Crucifixion site, dusk, interior	2 wooden benches, SR and SL	blues, shadows	•Domitian: teenage foot soldier •Marcus: early 50s, army captain •Vitruvius: mid-30s, army sergeant	•green fatigues and boots •generic khaki uniform with black boots with jacket •same as above with khaki tie	Stage crew dressed in fatigues brings set pieces and props onto stage in 2° blue while music plays.
Two	present, Jewish tavern, evening, interior	dark cracked walls, table SL, stained table-cloth, mugs, cups, several small round tables, candles, bowls of bread and nuts, wooden benches; door L to outside, door R to rest of tavern	dim while candles are lit, slow increase as candles provide more light	same as above	no jackets for Marcus and Vitruvius. Vitruvius carries kit bag.	Fade to blackout. Remove bread and candles in 2° blue, actors preset, pause, lights begin slow rise to full.
Three	same as scene 2, midday, interior	same as scene 2; remove bread, candles	full	same as above	same as above	Fade to blackout. Change in 2° blue. Blackout. Up with special.
Four	same, next morning	move jugs and cups lying on the floor	full, sunrise special	same as above	add green fatigue jacket to Domitian	

Budgeting

Based on the financial allocation of committees and boards, most evangelical drama directors have a prescribed budget for plays and musicals. Other directors may approach governing bodies of the church and request a specified amount necessary for a particular play. Others may have no financial backing whatsoever. Still others may have nearly unlimited resources in a fellowship where artistic expression is a source of premium Christian education, or where a fully equipped pro-grade theatre plant serves as the worship center.

Once the production plan and schedule have been hammered out, assign a deadline for the completion of designs and their corresponding budgets. Anticipate all expenses. List them specifically, such as royalties, theatre rental, director or staff salaries or stipends (when applicable), wood, hardware, paint, purchase or rental of lighting equipment, purchase or preparation of props, sound effects, rental and preparations of costumes, wigs, and makeup, advertising, programs, and tickets.

Many educational institutions have sponsors or patrons of the arts to supplement ticket sales. Professional theatres generate revenue from ticket sales alone. Most local churches have not developed such programs. You must evaluate your own situation and determine what is appropriate concerning a patron system or the sale of tickets. Ticket sales may have implications related to a church's nonprofit status. Check with a CPA.

If you have an ongoing drama ministry that regularly ministers in worship and evangelism, your church may not oppose ticket sales to larger events. In this case, prepare a ledger that lists on one side your anticipated income from all sources and on the other side all anticipated expenses. Ultimately, an accountant within your congregation should serve as a budget coordinator. Ask him to set up guidelines for financial procedures within which the production staff will operate, freeing up each staff member to concentrate on his aesthetic area. When funds can be dispersed, the staff can begin building the sets and costumes.

Designing

Once you have selected the designers, try collaborating with each other to accomplish a stylistic consistency within the production. Explain to the staff the overall approach to the play and ask designers if they have time to draw preliminary conceptions. The set designer is not the only person involved in the early stages. If money and time allow, engage all of the designers in the early stages. The lighting designer, who with the sound engineer is usually brought in at the last, can impact the visual presentation by creating scenic atmospheres with lighting. Sometimes lighting may enhance the scene more impressively than an actual set. It may also eliminate the expense of time and money in building three-dimensional sets.

Create an artistic rapport within the design group, which breeds creativity and spontaneity. Conduct brainstorming sessions in which every possible design concept is accepted. Begin eliminating possibilities only after all the options have been listed and the creative session has ended. It is important during the creative stages with the designers that you actively listen to the staff, holding their ideas and feelings in high esteem and considering them meritorious.

Now the designers can begin researching and creating sketches, color renderings, and set models that are in keeping with the interpretation of the play. This is optimum, maybe idealistic, but nevertheless generates a professional aura among the production staff. Keep a written record of the progress of the design team. Frequently correspond with the entire production staff through memos and letters, eliminating unnecessary meetings.

Set models may be a luxury you cannot expect. Consider the different strengths and temperaments of the design staff. Some designers may work best from pencil sketches, others from full-scale models. Allow them the freedom of their own methods.

In addition to the lighting designer and the sound engineer, consult the property master and the makeup coordinator in the earliest stages to produce organizational lists of their respective tasks. Property lists and actual props will be expanded as rehearsals progress. Procuring props early in the rehearsal period enables you to alter them as the need arises. On the other hand, makeup can be approved shortly before the last week unless special character makeup requires earlier attention.

Once the director and designers approve the major design decisions, you as the director are obligated to what has been agreed. Changes can be costly and may be interpreted as mercurial and demoralizing. This is not to restrain you from new discoveries during the rehearsal period but is to encourage you to do your homework early and not frustrate the staff with impulsive or whimsical leadership. With the production staff now in place, it is time to cast the play.

Casting

A cast may be the only production staff many drama directors have during the strategizing period. Since many local churches have yet to value the worth of communicating truth through drama, some directors feel blessed just to have enough people to fill the cast list. Consequently, survival is the keynote of our production process. Casting alone may determine whether a play will actually be produced.

To help create a comprehensive drama ministry in your local fellowship, try assembling a production staff first and then casting the play. Please refer to the section titled "Conducting Auditions" for further casting information.

PHASE THREE: BRING TO LIFE

Assuming the play has been cast, demands on your time will now intensify, as will the challenges to be a creative and inspiring leader. As the rehearsals begin, the hearts and minds of the participants will be stretched as everyone is grasped by the Spirit's teaching through the play. While emotions ebb and flow and nerves become exposed, your relationships with one another will distill into a stronger love and commitment. This is the very core of the drama ministry—the sanctification of the lives and worship attitudes of Spirit-led participants in the context of relationships. It is not a play that is being forged, but memories, and moments, precious to God and to His people. The drama director must not forget his first ambition: to equip disciples for ministry. In this creating period, rehearsals encompass the whole man: the actor and the Christian, the growth of a play and of the people.

PHASE FOUR: FUSION

In this final phase the whole becomes greater than the sum of its parts as the production nears its audience. You fine-tune the many subtleties of the production in accordance with the talent with which you are working.

Invite friends who have an objective view of the play to a final rehearsal. This may help you regain some of your objectivity now lost in the press of a thousand details. Is the plot line clear? Are characterizations believable? Is the pacing too slow? Is the lighting adequate?

Although you may have edited portions of the play weeks ago, there is no way of knowing for sure until you arrive in this final period. Intensify your attention to nuance. Challenge yourself to work through the final moment of the final performance. The final steps of fusion will be discussed later.

A timetable for these phases may look something like this:

Phase One: Studying and Theorizing	begins	with
Play Selection	at least 6 months	self
Analysis	before opening	self
Envisioning	of play	self
Phase Two: Strategizing		
Staffing	4-6 months	pastor
Budgeting	4-6 months	comptroller
Scheduling	4-6 months	secretary
Designing	4-6 months	designers
Casting	3-5 months	SM, AD
Phase Three: Bring to Life		
Rehearsals	3-5 months	SM, AD, cast
Construction	2-3 months	designers, crew
Phase Four: Fusion		
Technical Rehearsals	1-2 weeks	all
Dress Rehearsals	3-6 days	all
Final Presentation		all
Strike	that night or next day	all

As a final synthesis, a director's checklist of generalized tasks, conducted privately and publicly, is represented below. This list does not reflect a specific timetable since each director's needs and methods are different. Some procedures will not be applicable to all situations:

A DIRECTOR'S CHECKLIST

PRIVATE
- ✓ Spend time in prayer.
- ✓ Read scripts.
- ✓ Analyze needs relating to play selection.
- ✓ Select play.

- ✓ Prepare director's notebook.

PUBLIC
- ✓ Pray with a support group.

- ✓ Discuss ideas with a "play readers" group.
- ✓ Seek confirmation of play selection from group members (e.g., "play readers" group, deacons, elders, committee, etc.).

✓ Research the play.
✓ Analyze the action chronologically.
✓ Analyze the dramaturgical structure.
✓ Analyze the characters.
✓ Analyze the audience's perception.
✓ Determine any stylistic interpretations.
✓ Contact playwright for discussion.
✓ Prepare production outline for production staff.
✓ Prepare for auditions.

✓ Review audition notes and cast play as you see it.
✓ Prepare an ideal but realistic rehearsal schedule.

✓ Production staff meeting: design concepts.
✓ Conduct auditions with an audition panel, or select cast.
✓ Cast play with audition panel (NA if cast is preselected).
✓ Revise master rehearsal schedule with cast and staff.
✓ Read through play with entire cast.
✓ Production staff meeting: budget items; deadlines established.
✓ Meet with budget coordinator.
✓ Rehearse action: blocking phase.

✓ Analyze subtext and beats of acting moments to be rehearsed soon.
✓ Create the stage picture for each event.
✓ Create movement ideas for each action.

✓ Rehearse action: blocking phase.

✓ Rehearse action: blocking phase.

✓ Production staff meeting: progress reports.
✓ Meet with publicist.
✓ Conduct actor training workshops.
✓ Begin adding costumes and set pieces.
✓ Production staff meeting: final preparations.

✓ Prepare acting training sessions.

✓ Spend time in prayer.
✓ Evaluate nuance and subtleties of interpretation in acting.
✓ Evaluate nuance and subtleties of interpretation in directing.
✓ Evaluate nuance and subtleties of interpretation in visual design.

✓ Pray with support group.
✓ Rehearse action: polish phase.

✓ Rehearse action: polish phase.

✓ Rehearse action: polish phase.

✓ Production staff meeting: detail concerns.
✓ Meet with house manager: program design and ticket policies.

✓ Prepare private one-on-one final coaching sessions with each actor.

✓ Final coaching meeting with each actor.

✓ Transfer administration to stage manager.

✓ Spend time in prayer.

✓ Send thank-you notes.
✓ File all production materials.

✓ Oversee the integration of all production details as administrated by the stage manager.
✓ Pray with support group.
✓ Rehearse action without interruptions: tech week and dress rehearsals.
✓ Production staff meeting: performance details.
✓ Performances.
✓ Strike.

TWO

Scheduling Rehearsals
and
The Stage Manager

No one can prescribe the definitive rehearsal schedule for all directors and every play. There are a multitude of considerations belonging to each play regarding how many rehearsals will be scheduled. Every church has idiosyncratic schedules determining when and where rehearsals can occur. Most actors in the local church come to rehearsals after a long day at work, or on Saturdays or Sundays when they could be with their families. Therefore, the director and the stage manager work cooperatively with the cast and the church, determining what rehearsal commitment will be made to a given production. What worked for the last play may not be appropriate for the present project. Flexibility is the hallmark of scheduling rehearsals for every play, every scene, and every actor. Remember to tell your actors they are responsible to bring at least one sharp pencil to every rehearsal. They'll need it!

For purposes of this discussion, we will examine three approaches to the rehearsal plan. Each approach to scheduling is comprised of four phases: (1) the reading phase; (2) the blocking phase; (3) the polish phase; and (4) the audience phase. What differs in the comprehensive scheduling is the amount of time devoted to the first three phases.

The **reading phase** is the period of time the cast devotes to reading the script around a table, in a meeting room, or in someone's living room. The actors, director, and stage manager converse about matters of interpretation. Actors explore the script by concentrating on the text. Discussions embellish the reading as actors voice their questions about their character, the action, and what the author is trying to say. Some directors feel that a prolonged reading phase creates a positive anxiousness within the actors so that when they get to the blocking, they are highly motivated to create the movement that becomes the action.

The **blocking phase** labels the time when the actors and the director put the action of the play on its feet. This will be discussed in further detail in Part 2 within the section "Designing the Stage Composition." Suffice it to say here that the actors flesh out the characters as the action unfolds in the actor's movements. Some directors preblock each scene so meticulously that the actors come to rehearsal and are told when and where to move. Other directors work well with talented actors so that the movements of the actors naturally develop and are recorded by the stage manager as the permanent action of the play. Of course, the desired approach is a balance; improvisationally created kinetic movements for some of the action combined with the artistic manipulation of preblocked stage pictures.

The **polish phase** relates to a period of time when you detail specific scenes, actions, or moments in the play to maximize effect, perfect the timing, and clarify the meaning. Polish rehearsals are intended to revitalize the original energy in the play, which may have been present upon the director's first reading or subsequent discoveries in his research. This is a time when actors cut to the marrow of their acting ability, thereby deepening the impact of their physical interpretation of the playwright's words. But you should exercise discretion, for the polish rehearsals can discourage amateur actors who do not possess a sense of drive resident within more capable participants. Many people may not share your tireless zeal for rehearsal. Looking for details that cannot be produced by the level of ability of the actors is counterproductive. It may be better to move on to the run-throughs, technical and dress rehearsals.

The **audience phase** is self-explanatory. When all has been said and done, the play comes together for the audience's contemplation. The stage manager takes over most of the responsibilities for you in this phase.

Option A: Emphasis on Reading

Any one of the first three phases of the rehearsal period can be emphasized. The first option is distinguished by an emphasis on the reading period, designed for the advantage of the actors. The actors are advised against "giving a performance but instead . . . think about what the words mean and to hear each other's voice."[1] By concentrating on the text, each event in the play can be digested singularly, without thinking about characterization. During this period a desire to put words into actions wells up within the actor so that when the blocking rehearsals actually arrive, the actors' motivation for kinesthetic expression is at a peak.

With this emphasis, the blocking phase is relatively short because the actors have been primed to learn their movements quickly. Following a brief blocking phase, the director moves to polishing the scenes. With amateurs, and with church volunteers whose time is of the essence, this approach may be counterproductive as actors grow impatient for the seemingly all-important goal of memorizing lines and how, when, and where to move. On the other hand, if you have a cooperative cast who appreciates the value of this emphasis, a richness within the text and texture to the dramatic action may evolve that otherwise would not have surfaced. Perhaps this approach is best suited for plays dealing with highly intellectualized concepts or intensely involved relationships.

Option B: Emphasis on Blocking

A second comprehensive approach to rehearsal structure reflects an emphasis on blocking. The reading of the play may be scheduled for the first two or three rehearsals with the entire cast present. This may be the only time the whole company is assembled until run-throughs begin weeks later. After the read-through, scenes are broken down into manageable units. Only the actors involved in the scheduled scenes are required to attend subsequent rehearsals. Cast members put movement with their words immediately, memorizing actions with script and pencils in hand. This facilitates memorization since the actors may associate a particular feeling or phrase with a specific movement.

Your blocking ideas should be noted in your notebook. The rehearsals become a time of collaboration with the actors. By combining the dialogue with probing questions from the director, actors spawn physical interpretations of their lines, which become the desired blocking eventually noted in the stage manager's production notebook. Using this style, you should come to each rehearsal prepared to prompt the actors concerning their blocking. Rehearsals can be stimulating, provocative, and productive. Run-throughs become an opportunity for the actors to make the blocking natural, to make it their own as they marry movement to the memorized words. The desired effects of special moments in the play may emerge naturally. Consequently, polish rehearsals will focus on weak places that surface during run-throughs.

As with the first option, the actors must be intrinsically motivated to approach the blocking rehearsals in this manner. You may need to be an expert diplomat in resolving disparate interpretations to the satisfaction of the cast.

Option C: Emphasis on Polish

While you can spend a good deal of time around a table reading the script for all it's worth, or working with the actors so that they develop the movement, you may eliminate a cast read-through and entirely preblock movements to the actors. Movements and lines are memorized quickly, confident that cast members are capable of reading through the play on their own. Again, only those actors who are in a scheduled scene are required to attend a given rehearsal. Polish rehearsals begin fairly early in the rehearsal process as the actors investigate the dramatic moments in each scene, repeating the moments again and again until the ultimate interpretation is rendered. Having discarded the read-through and prescribed the blocking, polish rehearsals graduate to run-throughs several weeks prior to the audience viewing.

Sometimes the cast may comment that the play is being confusingly segmented by sectioning the script and requiring only a partial cast to attend specific rehearsals. Still, this is a practical approach to using wisely the volunteered time of an amateur cast. Experienced actors may enjoy the painstaking energy required to rehearse a scene over and over, while inexperienced ones may weary from the repetitions. This approach is also excellent for musicals in which songs are divided by short scenes, such as the senior choir's Christmas musical, a dramatized oratorio. This is an excellent approach for a collection of short sketches for a banquet or program.

Option D: Balance of All Options

The demands of the playscript, the ability of your actors, the amount of rehearsal time, and your own skill level will determine how much time you may devote to reading, blocking, polish, run-throughs, tech rehearsals, and dress rehearsals. Few directors in the drama ministry have the luxury of an extended reading phase, or the thrill of experimenting with blocking, or the patience to polish the action tediously. In fact, we must get to the run-through rehearsals fairly quickly because actors (especially the amateurs with which we work) need a sense of continuity and flow of the action. If you are in a situation where you can take advantage of the above options, you may find a quality of excellence and depth of insight otherwise illusive in the normal rush to produce a production.

COACHING SESSIONS

When actors are experiencing difficulty or when the size of the cast warrants it, individual coaching sessions need to be scheduled. There are times in a general rehearsal when an acting problem can be cleared up in a minimum of time and not at the expense of other cast members. When this is not possible, by all means schedule a coaching session. Key scenes between two or possibly three principals should automatically be scheduled for coaching.

Since each play, every cast, and all directors are different, allow the play, your personal approach to the production, and the experience level of the cast with which you are working to dictate the method you will use in scheduling rehearsals. An appropriate application of all three approaches to different scenes and actors may provide the balanced procedure to structuring rehearsals.

POSSIBLE REHEARSAL SCHEDULE FOR "THE PASSION"

1/12	Th	7-9:30	Read through	Full cast
1/18	W	7-10:00	Block Act I:1-3	Principals
1/22	Su	3-6:00	Block Act I:4-5	Mary, Solome, Servants
1/25	W	7-10:00	Review Act I	Full cast
1/29	Su	3-6:00	Review Act I	Full cast—off book
2/2	Th	7-9:00	Block Act II:1	Jesus, Judas, Peter
2/5	Su	3-6:00	Block Act II:2	Jesus, Disciples
2/9	Th	7-9:00	Block Act II:3	Full cast
2/12	Su	3-6:00	Review Act II:1-2	Jesus, Disciples
2/15	W	7-9:00	Review Act II:3	Full cast
2/19	Su	3-6:00	Review Act I	Full cast
2/23	Th	7-9:00	Review Act II	Full cast—off book
2/26	Su	3-6:00	Block Act III:1	Principals
3/1	W	7-9:00	Block Act III:2	Principals
3/5	Su	3-6:00	Block Act III:3-4	Full cast

3/9	Th	7-9:00	Review Act III:1-2	Principals
3/12	Su	3-6:00	Review Act III:3-4	Full cast—off book
3/15	W	7-9:00	Polish Act I	Full cast
3/19	Su	3-6:00	Polish Act II	Full cast
3/23	Th	7-9:00	Polish Act III	Full cast
3/26	Su	3-6:00	Polish Act III	Full Cast
3/29	W	7-9:00	Run Acts I and II	Full cast
4/1	Sa	10:00-Noon	Safety rehearsal	TBA
4/2	Su	3-6:00	Run Acts II and III	Full cast
4/5	W	7-9:00	Run-through	Full cast
4/9	Su	3-6:00	Run-through	Full company
4/10	M	6:30-10:30	Silent tech	Crew only, no cast
4/11	Tu	6:30-10:30	Technical rehearsal	Full company
4/12	W	6:30-11:00	Dress rehearsal	Full company
4/13	Th	6:30-11:00	Dress rehearsal	Full company
4/14	F	6:00 call	Performance	8:00 curtain
4/15	Sa	6:00 call	Performance	8:00 curtain
4/16	Su	4:00 call	Performance	6:00 curtain
4/17	M	6:00 call	Performance	8:00 curtain
			Strike	

Park Cities Christian Repertory
THE REHEARSAL SCHEDULE for *Luther,* by John Osborne

Reading Rehearsals

1st &
2nd
Weeks

1. Read entire play. Discuss meanings and problems of production.
2. Read Act 1 twice. Study interpretation and characterization.
3. Read Act 2 twice. Study interpretation and characterization.
4. Read Act 3 twice. Study interpretation and characterization.
5. Read entire play. Run play for total interpretation.

Blocking Rehearsals

3rd &
4th
Weeks

6. Block first half Act 1, set action, review blocking.
7. Block second half Act 1, set action, review first half Act 1.
8. Block first half Act 2, set action, review second half Act 1.
9. Block second half Act 2, set action, review first half Act 2.
10. Run Acts 1 and 2, review all blocking.
11. Block first half Act 3, set action, review blocking.
12. Block second half Act 3, set action, review Act 3.

5th &
6th
Weeks

13. Run Acts 1, 2, and 3, review all blocking.
14. Open period.

Polishing Rehearsals

15. Polish first half Act 1 by units, lines learned, review.
16. Polish second half Act 1 by units, lines learned, review Act 1.
17. Run Acts 2 and 3.
18. Polish first half Act 2 by units, lines learned, review.
19. Polish second half Act 2 by units, lines learned, review Act 2.

7th &
8th
Weeks

20. Run Acts 1 and 2, review all polishing.
21. Polish first half Act 3 by units, lines learned, review.
22. Polish second half Act 3 by units, lines learned, review Act 3.
23. Run entire play, review all polishing.
24. Open period, polish weak spots in Acts 1 and 2.
25. Run Acts 2 and 3.
26. Open period, polish weak spots in Act 3.

9th &
10th
Weeks

27. Run entire play.

Mounting Rehearsals

28. Silent technical rehearsal, crew only, no cast.
29. Technical rehearsal, continuity for technical effects.
30. Technical rehearsal, continuity.
31. Dress rehearsal.
32. Dress rehearsal.
33. Dress rehearsal.

THE STAGE MANAGER

Perhaps the most important colleague in your drama ministry will be your stage manager. In many ways, particularly in amateur settings, the stage manager may actually be an assistant director. The stage manager has specific duties and tasks of his or her own. Next to the actors, the single most important personnel resource you can have is a competent stage manager. To know that an administratively gifted person is organizing the details of the production, and doing a good job of it, releases you to concentrate solely on your directing and actor training responsibilities. When the performances have arrived, the stage manager assumes many responsibilities of the director and should almost be viewed as such.

It is strongly recommended that you purchase Lawrence Stern's invaluable work *Stage Management*. It contains all the information you will need to be a professional stage manager. It is an indispensable tool for directors as well. Following are a few organizational highlights of the important duties of a stage manager.

Prerehearsal Preparations

The function of a stage manger is to coordinate the operation of all the elements necessary to the efficient presentation of a play. This is the stage manager's first task and overriding goal. It is the stage manager's duty to see that all the details are covered. A stage manager lives by lists. The lists are constantly being added to, shortened, and altered. The stage manager should also construct his or her own production notebook, similar to the one constructed by the director.

Rapid Reference Page Tabs in a
Prompt Script/Production Notebook

Checklist
I-1
I-2
I-3
II-1
II-2
II-3
III-1
III-2
Cast
Schedules
Directory
Expenses
Lights
Sound
Props
Sets
Notes
Miscellaneous
Correspondence

Before rehearsals begin, the stage manager may need to:
- Be familiar with fire regulations and emergency numbers.
- Inspect the safety conditions of the rehearsal areas.
- Become familiar with the auditorium.
- Draw a ground plan of the stage.
- Investigate the electrical conditions and capacity of the auditorium.
- Draw a diagram of the existing lighting equipment.
- Continually keep a "to do" list.
- Construct a promptbook.
- Mark lighting, sound, and special effects cues in the script.
- Compose sound plot, lighting plot, costume plot, and effects plot for technicians.
- Construct a master calendar with the director.
- Schedule staff meetings with the director.
- Distribute rehearsal schedules.
- Arrange a call-board.
- Distribute and explain company rules.
- Coordinate audition forms.
- Organize cast, staff, and crew lists.

Rehearsal Period Administration

- Inventory scripts.
- Coordinate audition details (readings, forms, rooms, etc.).
- Oversee paperwork during auditions.
- Diagram preset information for each rehearsal (furniture for rehearsals).
- Prepare each rehearsal (implement above information).
- Prepare a running order (order of scenes and actors involved in each).
- Supervise technical personnel.
- Keep cast and director on time.
- Prepare and post duty roster (responsibilities of each cast and crew member).
- Oversee props.
- Complete scene shift diagrams (who, where, and when of set changes).
- Sustain order and discipline.

- Call rehearsal cues (speak aloud from script lighting and sound cues).
- Record blocking and movement in promptbook.
- Spike set pieces (place props in exact place for each rehearsal).
- Prompt.
- Announce rehearsal, costume, and publicity calls.
- Warn wandering actors that their scene is approaching.
- Time scenes.
- Post photo calls.
- Draft lighting sheet.
- Assist with take-in (bringing items out of storage into auditorium).
- Administrate technical rehearsals.
- Choreograph scene changes.
- Implement lighting diagram and add gels.
- Post sign-in sheet.
- Choreograph curtain call.
- Place curtain call lighting cues on lighting sheet.

Performance Practices

- Remind cast not to peek out at audience.
- Instruct cast to remain backstage once in costume and makeup.
- Run lighting cue check.
- Give 30-, 15-, and 5-minute calls.
- Concur with house manager.
- Cue show over headset.
- Supervise set changes.
- Immediately inspect results of all cues and changes.
- Time performances and curtain calls.
- Maintain props and sets.
- Be sensitive to cast morale.
- Monitor and diminish any unnecessary talking backstage during performance.

Postproduction

- Prepare and distribute strike plan (clearing and cleaning performing area).
- File all materials.[2]

► ► ► THREE ◄ ◄ ◄

Conducting Auditions

Next to the selection of a fine script, the greatest determining factor in the quality of the final presentation will be the cast. An off-Broadway adage has it that 90 percent of directing is casting. While this may not always be true, it is important to develop a sound approach to casting.

The goals of auditions are: (1) to learn as much as possible about the suitability of each applicant for a role: appearance, voice, personality, rightness for the highest moment of the part; (2) to learn as much as possible about the applicant's ability to perform: understanding of the role, imaginative range, flexibility, ability to take direction; (3) to determine whether or not a particular applicant will fit into the ensemble taking shape and whether this ensemble will best express the dramatic values of the script.[1]

There are three basic approaches to conducting auditions: (1) the general audition, frequently referred to as the "cattle call" in the professional theatre; (2) the private interview in which the actor presents prepared material in the form of a monologue and a song, followed by a discussion with the director and the assistant directors, and the stage manager; (3) audition by appointment, which is not an audition in the proper sense of the word but more of the director's appointment of a cast based on his intuition and an actor's desire to play a certain role. Each will now be discussed in turn.

General Auditions

While general auditions may be dehumanizing, they are an effective way of allowing those with a desire to be in the play to give their best shot. You may have auditionees prepare a scene or have them do a "cold" reading. The benefits of a prepared monologue may include a display of the actor's physical and emotional range and ability to approach the text. The disadvantage is that you do not know if the actor is flexible or creative. The advantage of the general audition is that all feel as if they were given a fair chance (especially among amateurs).

Each audition should last at least two to five minutes and include a scene involving two characters in dramatic conflict. You may have some individuals read for more than one part. It is suggested with this approach that you make decisions quickly. Allow interested individuals to sign up for a specific time so that no one has to waste time.

Audition Form

First Church

Name _____ Date _____

Address _____ Age _____ Sex _____

Phone (home) _____ (work) _____

Ht. _____ Wt. _____ Eyes _____ Hair color _____

Theatre experience:

List any rehearsal conflicts:

DO NOT WRITE BELOW THIS LINE

Vocal: 1 2 3 4 5   Stage presence: 1 2 3 4 5

quality—   Physical appearance—

pitch—   Imagination—

variety—

Roles considered for:

Another method for auditions is to select four to six or more two-person scenes that can be copied onto one 8½" x 11" sheet of paper. Mark out the lines that are not to be read. Label them by letter or number and have the auditionees pick up any of the copies and begin to rehearse the scenes in another room (see examples). Approximately 20 minutes after the auditions are scheduled to begin, the first auditionees should be ready. Allow all actors to audition as many times as they choose. Encourage them to prepare and present scenes for as long as the auditions are scheduled. Have several improvisations ready if you desire to discover more about the actors. Try to cast the play the same day or night, or early the next day. Use callbacks for musicals.

Private Interview

While the general audition allows you to see many prospects in shorter time, the private interview allows you to get to know the actors more personally. It becomes easier to probe into the actors' abilities concerning their understanding of a role and their flexibility as people. This may be important for large roles. You may examine the capabilities of their emotional and imaginative range as well as their ability to take direction. Since this is the method used in the professional theatre (except many musicals), use the private interview method for callbacks from the general auditions, or combine a private interview into the general audition schedule.

Offer auditions over the course of three or four days in a month and schedule each auditionee for a 30-minute period, 10 for the general audition, 10 for the improvisation, and 10 for the private interview. During the private interview, put the applicant immediately at ease and keep the conversation as informal as possible. Include questions about his or her personal testimony. This will assist you in preparing effective spiritual activities for the cast during the subsequent rehearsals. Discuss the play in general, then a specific role for which the actor has read.

Appointment

In many amateur, community, and church drama programs a director may not receive adequate response to an audition call. In this case it is not uncommon for the director to appoint talented, interested, or otherwise available people to specific roles. Even in this setting, an interview would be appropriate, especially if the project to be under-

Example of Audition Scenes

Scene A for 2 Men

STEVE: Look, I don't wanna get in the middle of this. You two have to work it out.

JIM: You're already in the middle of it. You always were.

STEVE: Right.

JIM: He knows where I am.

STEVE: Maybe he's waiting for you. Did you think of that?

JIM: Waiting for *me?* I didn't get arrested for drunk driving.

STEVE: You just got arrested for disorderly conduct.

JIM: That wasn't my fault. I was down there because of Todd. See? It all comes back to him. *He's* the one who decided to move out. *He's* the one who started acting weird when Barbara died.

STEVE: So?

JIM: So what?

STEVE: So who cares who did what? *(Moves to exit.)* I'm going up for his clothes. *(Exits.)*

JIM *(shouts after him):* I care. *(Paces restlessly for a moment.)* I'm going to see Dad tomorrow. You wanna go?

STEVE *(offstage):* What?

JIM *(shouting):* I said, I'm going to see Dad tomorrow. Do you want to go?

STEVE *(entering with a handful of clothes):* No. I don't think so. I was told I was the cause of his *last* stroke—wouldn't want to give him another.

JIM: Go with me, Steve.

STEVE: No.

JIM: Why not?

STEVE: It's not right. The timing's not right.

JIM: It's right. Come with me.

STEVE: No.

JIM: Why not?

STEVE: Why won't you come see Todd?

JIM: That's different.

STEVE: Why?

JIM: He's my son.

47

Snapshots & Portraits, PAUL MCCUSKER, Lillenas, 1989

Example of Audition Scenes

Scene B for 1 Man   1 Woman

~~MARK: I'd be glad to. (*Moves to exit, speaks to* SAMSON *in a deep, authorita-tive voice*) Let's roll, Kate. (MARK *and* SAMSON *exit.*)~~
~~MATTY: We'll be back in time for church.~~
~~CHARLIE: Thanks, Matty.~~
~~(MATTY *exits*)~~

JIM: We're going to church tonight?

CHARLIE: Christmas Eve service. Remember?

JIM: I don't, but that's all right. (*Begins taking off outerwear, etc.*) The place looks good, Charlie. Having Christmas here was a good idea.

CHARLIE: I'm glad you think so . . . since it was your idea.

JIM: Oh. It was, wasn't it?

CHARLIE: Jim, you know I'm not the kind of person to beat around the bush.

JIM: No, you're not. You might bludgeon the bush to death, but you don't beat around it. It's one of the things I always liked about you—you don't waste time. You get straight to the point.

CHARLIE: Are you involved with another woman?

JIM (*pause*): Maybe you should try beating around the bush sometime. How could you ask me that question?

CHARLIE: Things have changed between us, and I've heard rumors about you and Gwen whatshername. I added two and two and came up with that question.

JIM: What kind of rumors?

CHARLIE: How many different kinds are there? I want a direct answer.

JIM: Are you sure you want to talk about this now—on Christmas Eve?

CHARLIE: Yes. (*Beat*) No. (*Closes eyes to compose herself*) Wait. I'm afraid.

JIM: Afraid?

CHARLIE: I've spent weeks playing out this scene in my mind and now that I'm here, I'm afraid that it won't end the way I want it to.

JIM: How do you want it to end, Charlie?

CHARLIE: You take me in your arms and tell me everything's OK and we'll go on living as we have for over 20 years.

(CHARLIE *looks at him—as if expecting* JIM *to play out the scene that way. He doesn't move. He stands silently.*)

CHARLIE: That's not how this scene is going to end, is it?

Family Outings, PAUL MCCUSKER, Lillenas, 1988

taken is a full-length production. It is best, of course, to cast the most talented actors in the longest and demanding roles. However, if you need to look toward the future, you may consider ways to stretch the talents and capabilities of other actors to increase their usefulness later.

NOTIFICATION OF AUDITIONS

Place a notification of the audition dates in various communiques of your church. Experts in advertising say that people must see something three times before it gets their attention. Schedule at least three notifications for the audition dates. Make available copies of the script or score through the church office. Include specific information such as: name of production, dates of presentation, rehearsal schedule (optional), director and personnel committed to production, cast of characters, time of audition, place, what will be expected at the audition, what to wear, relevant telephone numbers for further information.

Upon arrival at the audition site, have the actors complete an audition information form, giving you pertinent facts about each applicant. Along with name, address, and telephone number, you will want to know about previous experience, including the names of the plays, roles, and the approximate dates and places of the performances. Height, weight, and color of hair may be important considerations when thinking in terms of the final cast ensemble. Allow a place where they can inform you of specific roles for which they want to audition. Also include on the form a place where they may indicate their ability to meet the tentative rehearsal schedule. Provide space at the bottom of the sheet for your notes and the notes of the audition panel (if applicable). If your general auditions involve 75 or more, you may want to require a photograph of each auditionee or videotape the auditions.

Although the director needs to make the final casting decisions, it is wise to have an audition panel or committee observing each audition. Ask three or four people whose opinions you value and who work well together to look at the auditions objectively, recording on each audition form their impressions of the applicant. Each member of the panel should be familiar with the play or musical, the cast, the demands of the leading roles, and what specific details, if any, the director will be looking for regarding the casting of the major roles. This information will be valuable later when you meet to cast the play.

Director's Checklist for Auditions

Your Options for Auditions Are:
- "Cold" readings
- Interviews
- Improvisations/theatre games
- General tryouts
- Rehearsed scenes
- Hybrid of any of the above

Your Audition Process Is:
- Efficient
- Fair
- Clear
- Gives all actors maximum opportunity

Your Records:
- Give a clear picture of each actor
- Differentiate between all actors
- Contain coded information about each actor's abilities

Qualities to Evaluate:
- Physical appearance
- Age
- Vocal quality and diction
- Sense of movement
- Flexibility and imagination
- Stage presence and projection

Common Errors:
- Good reader but poor actor
- Poor reader but fine actor
- Director's lack of script study
- Director's preconceptions of physical interpretation of each character

FUNDAMENTAL CONSIDERATIONS FOR CASTING

During the applicant's audition, you will be examining appearance, voice, personality, and ability. By researching the play and analyzing the script, you may know in general terms qualities you are looking for in each character, enabling you to eliminate certain actors immediately and making the casting process easier.

The first fundamental consideration is the applicant's **physical suitability** to a role. Physical appearance relates to the actor's appropriateness to a given part and overall contribution to the ensemble at large. This includes the actor's posture and gestures. The dynamic range of the actor's physical and emotional abilities determines how the actor will interpret the character. Virtually any actor can be cast in any role as long as his or her voice and appearance do not fracture the dramatic worth of the character and the script, and he or she has talent.

The second fundamental consideration is the actor's **voice**. The voice must be understood, suited to the role, and capable of projecting through the auditorium. Probably the most important observation about an actor's voice is his or her ability to be understood. There are few things more annoying than not being able to understand an actor. An actor's voice must also be pleasing to the ear. An audience grows weary of 45 minutes to two hours of a strident voice. Many of the emotions of a character and much of the action of the play are carried on the actor's voice through enunciation, accent, strength, and nuance. In the Western tradition of acting training, the development of the actor's body and voice comprise a four-year program. Obviously, the body and the voice are the actor's greatest instruments.

Third, an actor's personality offstage may not necessarily be the same **personality as onstage**. Certain characteristics may alter when an actor steps onstage. A women who is demure and unassuming offstage may have a powerful stage presence. Stage presence is that unexplainable quality that makes you want to watch the person while he or she is onstage. Sometimes it is referred to as charisma. But it is more than charisma, because charisma can be manufactured. Stage presence is natural. It is either there, or it isn't. The varying degrees of stage presence among actors become evident during the audition.

You need to be concerned with the onstage personality and its effect on the audience. Now since each character in a play has at least one crucial scene, you can evaluate major personality qualities of each character in his or her respective climactic scene. Consider what effect the onstage personality of an actor will have on the audience as it synthesizes with the character's crucial scene. If the onstage personality of the actor is well-suited to the qualities of the character during his crucial scene, then the actor is right for the part. If not, the actor should not be considered for that role. Don't forget, as a director in a drama ministry, you also have the privilege of relating to the offstage personality as you minister through fellowship in God's Word, prayer, good deeds, and accountability.

Fourth, **acting experience** is helpful. Few people in the local church today have had extensive acting training. Congregations that have professional Christian actors within their fellowship can communicate God's truth in ways many other local churches cannot. Keeping this in mind, one of the objectives of this text is to help the drama director address this area of deficiency. Common sense makes it obvious that the most talented actors are given demanding roles. The only time this may not be the case is when the director has the future in mind. In this instance, the director may choose a less experienced actor for a leading role to help him or her grow through new challenges and stretching ventures, in preparation for forthcoming leading roles.

Fifth, ask each actor if there are any rehearsal **schedule conflicts** or limitations before you post the final cast list.

In summary, do not cast totally inexperienced actors in long, demanding roles, or anyone in a role that will make him or her look silly or absurd. Cast on the basis of a person's onstage personality rather than offstage personality, while not casting too far away from type. Do not cast on the basis of the readings alone, but on the whole of the interview and the actor's evidence of imagination. Although casting the play may pale in comparison to staging every second of the action, "mistakes at the casting stage can rarely be eradicated by even the most brilliant actor coaching or staging."[2]

PART II

FROM WORDS
TO PICTURES

▶▶▶ FOUR ◀◀◀

Analyzing the Playscript

When you think of all the responsibilities that go into directing a production, it is easy to understand why Christian drama is not prevalent in the local church. The overall process requires either a small group of specifically talented and dedicated people or a director who has enough experience, energy, and time to accomplish the task alone. The administrative imperatives alone require hours of concentration.

If casting the show reflects your interpretation of the play, this implies you have spent a good deal of time researching and analyzing the script. In a society where speed and change are hallmarks, one is hard-pressed to find a drama director who will begin work on a play far in advance of its production meetings and auditions. Complicating the issue is the fact that volunteer drama directors are usually engaged in a career and shaping a family, making it even more difficult to find the time for preparation. Yet, preparation is the key to excellent directing, and few preparatory tasks require as much time as analyzing the script.

Tools for Analysis

In keeping with the practical emphasis of this book, analyzing the script will be examined from the perspective of what you can directly apply to the production. Many volumes have addressed the literary analysis of the playscript. You are encouraged to study these sources further.

You may want to have dictionaries and materials for historical information as well as reference books on common allusions and theatre subjects, such as:

Dictionaries
   Webster's New World Dictionary

A Dictionary of English Pronunciation
A Concise Encyclopedia
A Dictionary of Slang and Unconventional English
A Dictionary of First Names
A Dictionary of Foreign Terms

Historical Materials

The Timetables of History
20,000 Years of Fashion
Webster's Biographical Dictionary
Brockett's *Essential Theatre*

General Allusions

Bartlett's *Familiar Quotations*
A Dictionary of Phrase and Fable
A Companion to English Literature

Theatrical Subjects

A Concise Encyclopedia of the Theatre
A Dictionary of Theatrical Terms

Other Sources

There may be several editions of the same play that would aid in its interpretation. Compare and contrast the different editions and their perspectives.

Translations may also be helpful. Some plays have several English translations from which to choose. If you combine portions of various translations, make sure that you have assembled an even and seamless text for the action of the play.

Any biblical play set in its historical context will be steeped in its cultural setting. Therefore, seek as many **historical sources** as you can when reading and analyzing the play. You may begin the first rehearsal with a discussion of the world of the play: the geography of the setting, daily life, music, and manners and customs. Discover numerous visual materials that can be shared with the cast concerning the people of the age and their civilization (in addition to costumes and sets of previous productions). Drama based on historical figures may require you to read biographies and other source materials. In a passion play, for instance, it would be difficult for a director to render fully the tension between Jesus and the Pharisees without a thorough knowledge of the historical background of Jewish customs, ceremonies, social life, Temple regulations, and the judicial processes during the Passover holiday.

Critical sources provide a considerable body of auxiliary knowledge about the play. Unless it is a new work, in which case there would be no critical or descriptive material, you may uncover essential facts from the author's preface, interpretive recommendations, or any interviews. University presses frequently print information about most dramatic authors. Be advised that information from critical sources does not generate creativity for the actors. Rather it is a supplemental utensil for the director's craft.

Finally, consult other churches about their production of the play. Obtain photographs, production notebooks, director's notes, and talk to people who have worked on the play or have been in it. Discuss interpretational questions. If the **playwright** is accessible, investigate his or her impressions of the work, or whether he or she has worked on other productions of the play. Ask the playwright, "What do you really want to say with this work?" "How much of the play is autobiographical and why?" "What changes within audience members do you seek with this material?" Occasionally you may communicate with the playwright during the rehearsal period about questions that may arise.

First Read-through

Your script must contain many notations. Besides blocking diagrams, the margins of your script will carry light and sound cues, prop reminders, interpretation notes, and more. Construct a director's notebook similar to the stage manager's promptbook as shown on page 30.

Write notes in pencil since they are likely to be revised. Mark cues in your script according to a system that works best for you. Some directors use colored pencils, others use rulers, others scribble. Opposite each page of script will be a ground plan upon which you can record the blocking.

The first read-through of the selected play should be accomplished in one uninterrupted sitting. Record in your notebook any questions or feelings that may arise through your reading as well as how you suspect the audience may react to the scenes. Dispel any preconceptions you may have about the material and let the play speak for itself. Follow these key points during the first reading:

1. Examine the cast list and layout of the script.

2. What contributions are made by the prefatory material, stage directions, weather, social customs, names, or anything else that affects the setting or events in the play?

3. Use pencil to record all impressions.

4. Ask yourself a lot of questions and record all of them. As answers come up, record them also.

5. Believe everything you read.

6. Establish the settings for offstage events.

7. Read for information, not empathy.

As you read the play, discover and record the following structural elements contained in the action of a play, such as:

Plot: the complete unified dramatic action described in the script.

Action: a complete sequence that has a definite beginning, middle, and end.

Beginning: point at which nothing else in the action has gone before.

End: point at which nothing else in the action is left to follow.

Event: a happening that changes the relationships among the characters or between the characters and their world.

Cause: an event that requires a response for another character.

Effect: an event that occurs in response to or as a result of a previous event.

Empowering event: an event that does not contribute directly to the chain of cause and effect but sets up situations in which dynamic events can proceed.

Dynamic event: part of the chain of cause and effect that moves the action forward from the beginning to the end.

Sequence: order of events in the action as discovered by the characters and the audience.

Situation: all the known circumstances preceding any moments in the course of the play.

Unity: the assumption on the part of the reader that everything in the script belongs there so that all parts fit together.

Structural setting: time and place as viewed by audience.

Situational setting: time and place at which each event in the course of the action occurs.

ANALYZING THE STRUCTURE OF THE PLAY

Audiences enjoy a sense of structure. They are accustomed to Western civilization's structural elements of exposition, inciting incident, development (or rising action), crisis, climax, and denouement of a play. **Exposition** is the precipitating context or background information of the action before the emergence of a driving force, set off by some **inciting incident**. The **driving force** is the vehicle that develops the **rising action**. Resistance between the driving force and other forces in the play generates the **crisis** moments, ultimately leading to the **climax**, the crux of the dramatic action and the high point of the play. **Denouement** comes from a French word meaning "unraveling" and labels the point when the play unwinds as the issues resolve. Examine the action and identify these major structural elements.

ANALYZING WITH THE AUDIENCE IN MIND

Audiences also enjoy a sense of involvement. Simply stated, the basic experience of the audience viewing a play involves the elements of expectation, unpredictability, and gratification. When an audience member's expectation of the action in the play is fulfilled, a sense of gratification emerges. But for dramatic interest an audience connects with the play when something unpredictable interrupts their sense of expectation, giving life to new expectations and opportunities for gratification. This cyclical process of expectation, unpredictability, and gratification continues as long as the play is well written and the audience remains involved with the action. A section of your analysis should consider these essential ingredients of the play's action.

On a more specific level, audience members deepen their involvement in the play performance by identifying with the characters through:

Understanding: the audience accepts a character.

Attraction: the audience likes a character.

Empathy: the audience shares in the experience of the character's situations.

Sympathy: the audience agrees wholeheartedly with the character.

Hope: the audience desires a specific outcome for a character.

Personality traits: qualities attractive or repulsive to the audience.

Opponents: the audience is driven closer to likable characters who are opposed by less honorable characters.

Status: a character of weaker status usually gains the empathy of the audience.

Morality and Motivation: virtuous motives make a character attractive to the audience.

ORGANIZING AND RECORDING YOUR OBSERVATIONS

Now synthesize your analysis by composing a one-sentence description of what happens in the play. Include in this sentence the main character, who is the protagonist, the antagonist, the nature of the conflict, and the outcome of the play's dramatic plot. This is called the **central dramatic action.**

It is generally believed that every play is about one character and one character alone. Although the play may include the action of a variety of characters, for the text analysis stage, the director needs to select the one character on which the play revolves. This is the true **protagonist**, the character who has the greatest impact on the central dramatic action of the play.

Divide the play into three major **units**, following the progression of the conflict. In the first unit the conflict is initiated. In the second unit it unfolds, and in the third unit the conflict is resolved. Give a title to each unit in the form of a core verb that best describes the development of the dramatic action. Break down each unit into smaller subdivisions using additional core verbs to describe the dramatic action, identifying **minor climaxes** and **beats** within the character's action.

Within each of these units there will be a **major climax.** As the conflict between the protagonist and the antagonist progresses, there will be a moment of greatest intensity.

Write a statement that expresses what the playwright is saying about life and the human condition. This sentence should be a universal, irreducible principle in the most general of terms. This is called the **spine**, or theme, of the play.

One technique you may want to use is constructing a **rhythmical wave**. The rise and fall of the unfolding conflict can be graphed in a linear fashion, revealing the ebb and flow of the intensity of the action, and the peaks of the climactic moments.[1]

Director's Analysis of *Family Outings*

Central Dramatic Action

Charlie retreats to a remote, dilapidated cabin, purchased by her husband, Jim, where their family bonds are tested and strengthened by unexpected tragedy, dangerous personal transparency, and the recognition of their need to remain completely dependent on God.

Protagonist

Charlie

Major Units

    I. Charting the Roads (pp. 9-19)

    II. Escapes Lead to Meetings (pp. 19-55)

    III. Taking the Alternate Route (pp. 55-59)

Inciting Incident

Jim: "Seal it." (p. 18)

Subunits

    A. Setting Out (pp. 9-13)

    B. Establishing the Territory (pp. 14-18)

    C. Detour I (L & B) (pp. 18-19)

    D. Working on Things (pp. 19-22)

    E. Recognizing Changes (p. 22, after Mark's exit, p. 24)

    F. Sharing Dreams (pp. 24-27)

    G. Deciding Whether to Face Facts (pp. 28-31)

H. Taking Dreams Back (pp. 31-34)

I. Confrontation (p. 34, light change, p. 39)

J. Detour II (L & B) (pp. 39-40)

K. Holiday Surprise (pp. 40-42)

L. Banging the Pipes (pp. 43-51)

M. It'll Be All Right (pp. 51-55)

N. Detour III (L & B) (p. 55)

O. Working at It (pp. 57-59)

Major Climax

Jim: "Then you'll forgive me?"
Charlie: "Yes. Will you forgive me?"
Jim: "Yes." (pp. 54-55)

Spine

In our attempt to escape from our problems and failings, the Lord will inevitably lead us to confront them directly.

Rhythmical Wave

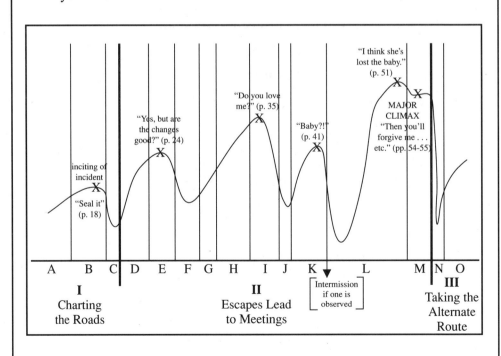

ANALYZING THE ACTION OF THE PLAY

With much of the broad analysis complete, begin analyzing each unit of action. This is an excellent method for you to prepare for each rehearsal, keeping your understanding of the script fresh and accurate. Begin with the end of the play and work backward in a meticulous manner following these six steps:

1. Discover the last action.
2. Identify its immediate cause.
3. Evaluate the immediate cause: (a) Is it sufficient to make the event happen the way it does? (b) Would this event happen without the immediate cause?
4. Backtrack through the script as described above, beginning with the last action and ending with the beginning action. Chart the interlocking and overlapping sequence of cause-and-effect actions.
5. Determine empowering events from dynamic events.
6. Evaluate: (a) Does your description account for the presence of all the characters in the play? (b) Are all the events accounted for? (c) Does the production staff agree? (optional)

ANALYSIS OF CHARACTER ACTION:
OBJECTIVES AND INTENTIONS

Each character has a goal in the play's action. Obstacles stand in the way of this goal, so the character comes up with a series of objectives to overcome these obstacles. Obstacles can be other characters, elements of nature, situations, or physical barriers. When the objective is not met, the character devises other intentions to get around the obstacle until the obstacle is conquered or the character gives up on that objective and decides to pursue another one. Each objective is made up of changing intentions. Numerous intentions make up many objectives, which make up the character's goal.

There are four steps to discovering the intentions and objectives of a character. Begin at the end of the script and:

1. Find the last character event described in the script.
2. Identify the stimulus for this event.
3. Determine the response that precedes step 2.
4. Repeat steps 2-4 for each event and character in the script.

Label each character's scene with the character's objective, "to . . ." Identify all intentions within a single objective as the scene progresses.

Excerpt from "Doors"
In Season and Out (p. 69), Larry Enscoe
Lillenas, 1985

"The <u>Final Entrance</u>"

COLLIN: I asked you not to come in here. Why didn't you listen?

VERN: You . . . you're an old man—

COLLIN: Your perception amazes me.

VERN: I was begging you? I thought you had all the answers. (*Going to him*) I was trusting you!

COLLIN (*mustering himself*): I'm warning you, Vern, don't try and take me, please please just leave me alone. (*Small pause*.) I couldn't stand to—find out that you were wrong—that there wasn't a door. I'm too old for another heartache, don't you see? I know this place too well. I couldn't try to leave it.

VERN: You've been here all these years and you couldn't do it. You've had years! You've been tryin' so long you made staying your choice.

COLLIN (*withdrawing*): Vern . . . please . . . don't make me . . . (*sighing*) Don't you think I've heard all this before? I just can't believe there is really something there—

VERN: So you convinced yourself there's not. And now you can't go.

COLLIN: It's not so bad. Don't lots of people take this and don't question it? They don't kick and claw, do they? They just accept it. They can be happy, can't they? You just—stay away from the windows. (VERN *steps closer.* COLLIN *yells.*) No! Don't show me what I know can't be there!

VERN: But you been lyin'. You're still lyin'.

COLLIN (*moving out of his range*): Vern, I won't go. (*Pause*) Just let me stay here. (*Quickly*) Look, I need time to . . . think it all over, huh? Let me think it over! (*Long pause.*)

VERN (*handing him the pamphlet*): Here's the paper with the directions to the door. But if you're not outa here in just a little while I'm comin' in after you, you understand that?

COLLIN: Sure, Vern.

VERN: We all hate this place, ain't that right, Collin?

COLLIN (*without conviction*): Of course . . . you're right . . . we all hate this place . . . (VERN *smiles and goes. The lights begin a slow fade.* COLLIN *sits on the bed and watches the TV for a moment. He looks at the pamphlet. He looks up at the window. With expression.*) God, you know how I hate this place!

(*And the stage is in darkness.*)

TEXT ANALYSIS
Example of Analysis of a Unit of Action

<u>Step 1</u>
• Structural setting: in Collin's room

• Situational setting: after Vern's entrance into Collin's "space," before Vern's final departure

<u>Step 2</u>
• Unit of script described as an event, "The_____"

<u>Step 3</u>
• Objectives of characters stated as "I want to . . ."

COLLIN: "I want to be left alone."
VERN: "I want to take him with me."

<u>Step 4</u>
• Subevent

The Giving of the Word

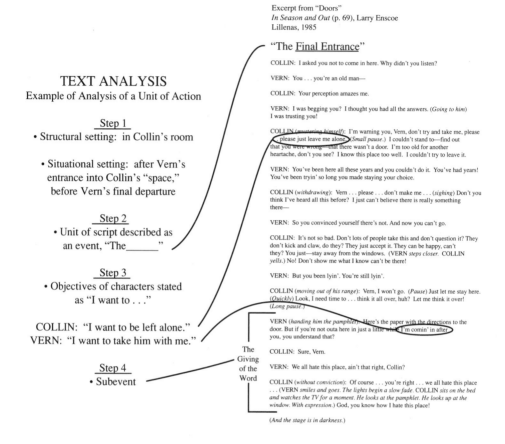

Excerpt from "Doors"
In Season and Out (p. 69), Larry Enscoe
Lillenas, 1985

TEXT ANALYSIS
Example of Analysis of Character Action

Identifying causes by working backward through the playscript, focusing on the *causes* of character action.

"The <u>Final Entrance</u>" (title of this event)

VERN: You've been here all these years and you couldn't do it. You've had years! You've been tryin' so long you made staying your choice.

COLLIN (*withdrawing*): Vern . . . please . . . don't make me . . . (*sighing*) Don't you think I've heard all this before? I just can't believe there is really something there—

VERN: So you convinced yourself there's not. And now you can't go.

COLLIN: It's not so bad. Don't lots of people take this and don't question it? They don't kick and claw, do they? They just accept it. They can be happy, can't they? You just—stay away from the windows. (VERN *steps closer.* COLLIN *yells.*) No! Don't show me what I know can't be there!

Final indictment identifies Collin's rationalization.

VERN: But you been lyin'. You're still lyin'.

COLLIN (*moving out of his range*): Vern, I won't go. (*Pause*) Just let me stay here. (*Quickly*) Look, I need time to . . . think it all over, huh? Let me think it over! (*Long pause.*)

Caused by

VERN (*handing him the pamphlet*): Here's the paper with the directions to the door. But if you're not outa here in just a little while I'm comin' in after you, you understand that?

COLLIN: Sure, Vern.   **Patronizing answer**

VERN: We all hate this place, ain't that right, Collin?

Collin's apathy causes Vern's exit.

COLLIN (*without conviction*): Of course . . . you're right . . . we all hate this place . . . (VERN *smiles and goes. The lights begin a slow fade.* COLLIN *sits on the bed and watches the TV for a moment. He looks at the pamphlet. He looks up at the window. With expression.*) God, you know how I hate this place!

Beat

(*And the stage is in darkness.*)

Continue to work through each event from the end of the play to the beginning

Subtext between these two sentences; marked by a beat

Exit causes subtext

Subtext causes final dialogue

IDENTIFYING THE BEATS IN A SCENE

Many times a character will change objectives quickly. A change in objective or intention is usually marked by a beat. Although "beats" are essential for an actor studying the character, it is also good for you as the director to be aware of the beats within a scene. A beat is a section of a scene during which the character pursues a single intention or objective, identified by the character introducing a slightly different topic, changing an activity, or changing an emotional state. Again, a step-by-step process will enable the director to discover beats within each scene:

1. Determine where a beat occurs in the character's action.

2. Form a statement that explains what actually happens to encourage the character to adjust or alter the intention during a beat.

3. Repeat this process for each beat discovered in the character's plot.[2]

Example of Beats

Excerpt from
Family Outings (p. 36), McCusker, Lillenas, 1988

JIM: Are you sure you want to talk about this now—on Christmas Eve?

CHARLIE: Yes. (*Beat*) No. (*Closes eyes to compose herself*) Wait. I'm afraid.

JIM: Afraid?

CHARLIE: I've spent weeks playing out this scene in my mind and now that I'm here, I'm afraid that it won't end the way I want it to.

JIM: How do you want it to end, Charlie?

CHARLIE: You take me in your arms and tell me everything's OK and we'll go on living as we have for over 20 years.

Beat (CHARLIE *looks at him—as if expecting* JIM *to play out the scene that way. He doesn't move.* He stands silently.)

CHARLIE: That's not how this scene is going to end, is it?

JIM: No, Charlie. Not this time.

CHARLIE (*toughening up*): Then you better answer the question.

Character (CHARLIE) shifts intention or objective (as indicated by the beat). Beats indicate intense subtext, and are frequently expressed by silence.

FIVE

Designing the Stage Composition

As stated earlier, it is the aim of this book to facilitate amateur drama producers and directors in successfully presenting a well-directed dramatic piece. In order to accomplish this, every director needs to develop his or her skill in designing the visual picture on stage. The elements of this visual picture include composition, picturization, gesture, movement, rhythm, and style.

Before you begin "painting," the scenic elements on the stage need to be mapped out. This is called a ground plan. You need to create your own ground plan, which is an arrangement of furniture and all the pieces of a set (windows, doors, etc.). The ground plan indicates the orientation of the set; either it is designed with the axis parallel to the footlights or it is set at an angle (raked). Designate locations around the set

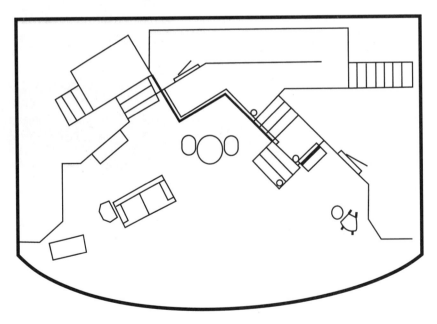

unseen by the audience, e.g., which door leads to the kitchen, outside, etc. Furniture arrangement should conform to the axis of the set, creating at least two or more distinct playing areas. Place these acting areas on different planes and give the areas an apparent light source. Do not obscure the audience's view of windows and doors where important action may take place. The sight lines of a ground plan are determined by sitting in the farthest left front row seat and farthest right front row seat (horizontal) and from the front row center seat to the farthest backseat center (vertical).

BLOCKING

The term "blocking," frequently used for creating the composition, refers to all the movements and positions of the actors on stage. Blocking is used to create clarity, focus, behavior, special effects, aesthetic effects, abstract effects, symbolic patterns, and variety. It is the general term for any movement on stage.

Clarity can easily be achieved by keeping the speaking actor's face visible, by isolating the beats in the scene and blocking accordingly, and by discussing the meaning of the action with the actors. If in your blocking you are able to isolate principal actors and define each movement and position in terms of its intention, then clarity will begin to be realized. Solicit evaluations from friends to check the clarity of the blocking.

Discover clues in the script that give focus to the character. Translate the words into visual clarity through blocking techniques such as: a character being pointed at, a character speaking, a character facing the audience, a character moving, a character who is isolated, a character who is moving in a pattern different from others, a character who is more brightly lit or in a more interesting part of the stage, or a character who is downstage.

Blocking also **creates behavior** that is not specifically called for in the script but nevertheless adds life to the play experience. Consider using obstacles that create behavior as suggested by the setting or by the characters. Create behavior that contrasts the inner action of a scene. The inner action of a scene is the truth of the emotional motivations as discovered in the character's intentions and designated by beats. Exercise judgment against gimmicky behavior.

Additionally, blocking assures **honesty and truth** because your

...on is to make internal emotions become external actions. The inner action of the play is a synthesis of three elements: (1) what the character wants to do (intention); (2) why the character wants to do it (motivation); (3) what the character is thinking when he or she does it (subtext). Review the discussion of beats from your analysis of the play. You reveal the inner action by blocking actors according to their emotional state and interpersonal relationship with other characters. Your blocking should be a natural product of the text. The script guides your decisions for actor movements and positions.[1]

Stage Terms

Blocking involves the use of common stage terms. In 1545, an architect and painter "raked" his stage so that it was flat near the audience but rose in a slant toward the back. To this day, we direct actors downstage (D) if moving toward the audience and upstage (U) if moving away. The downstage plane is considered stronger than the upstage plane. Stage left (L) and stage right (R) are from the actor's perspective, not the audience's. Stage right is thought to be stronger than stage left since the Western eye travels from left to right. Center stage

Tonal Qualities of Stage Planes

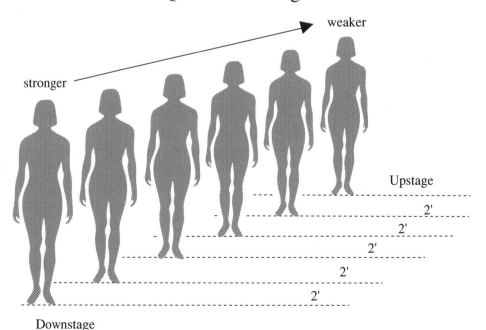

(C) is the strongest position onstage, all other things being equal. These conventions are only generalizations and may be altered by the action that is taking place or by numerous other variations of blocking.

Directors must be aware that an actor's body has a changing tonal quality as he or she moves onstage. A "full front" position is directly facing the audience and is the strongest. A "one-quarter" turned away is weaker than a full front but stronger than "profile." The "three-quarter" turned away (or "three quarters closed") is weaker still, while the "full back" position may be the weakest or the strongest, depending on the situation.

Tonal Qualities of Body Positions

Full Back
(weakest, or strongest)

Three-quarter
Closed Right
(weaker)

Three-quarter
Closed Left
(weaker)

Right Profile

Left Profile

One-quarter
Open Right
(strong)

One-quarter
Open Left
(strong)

Full Front
(strongest)

In addition to the planes of the stage and the tonal quality of the actor's body position, the height of an actor above the stage floor is an essential part of blocking. Lying on the floor, sitting on the floor, sitting in a chair, sitting on the arm of the chair, standing, standing on steps or at the height of a stairway are the levels onstage from weakest to strongest. Again, this generalization can be altered by the height of other actors. For instance, if all actors are standing at the highest point but one actor is lying on the floor, the strongest focus will be on the actor lying on the floor.

Tonal Qualities of Stage Levels

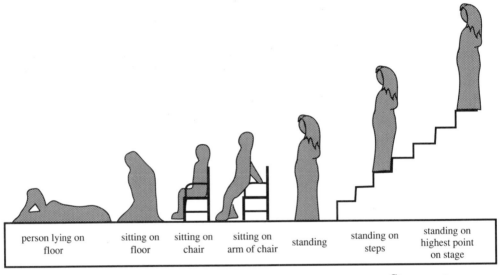

| person lying on floor | sitting on floor | sitting on chair | sitting on arm of chair | standing | standing on steps | standing on highest point on stage |

Weakest ———————————————————— Strongest

Your approach to blocking a play will be determined by the demands of the text and the level of experience of the actors. If you are an experienced director, well-trained actors may work best in an environment of improvisation whereby you allow the actors to create the blocking in unstructured but highly creative rehearsal sessions. A sophisticated comedy, on the other hand, fraught with physical activity, may require painstaking planning. It is usually best, if you lack experience, to rely heavily on blocking the action prior to rehearsal:

Ordinarily beginners are cautioned to preblock. First, the rehearsal time is limited. Until a director is fast enough to come up with blocking spontaneously, much time could be lost in pondering blocking decisions . . . the successful attainment of directorial objectives takes careful thinking . . . if the blocking is to achieve clarity and telling effects, the director almost certainly has to plan it.

Experienced directors tend to do much gross preblocking, often in their heads with a note or two in their promptbooks. Entrances and exits are plotted, key scenes are diagrammed, certain effects are planned, and suggestions for behavior at various moments are at the ready. The scene is blocked roughly and then refined, changed, and supplemented during the course of rehearsals. This is probably the most common method of blocking in use today.[2]

COMPOSITION

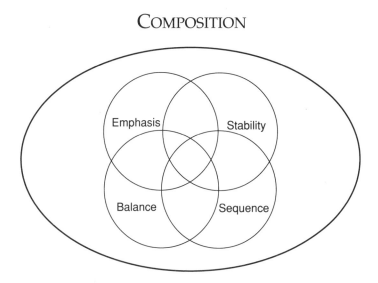

Theatre professor Francis Hodge defines composition as "the physical arrangement of actor-characters in a ground plan for the purposes of discovering dramatic action and of illustrating it in the simplest possible way through emphasis and contrast." Two other theatre professors, Robert Cohen and John Harrop, define it as the "rational arrangement of people in a stage group through the use of emphasis, stability, sequence, and balance, to achieve an instinctively satisfying clarity and beauty." Composition embodies a battery of techniques that aid the director in clarifying the action in the play. It refers not only to the behavior of actors on the stage but also to the overall scenic look of the play. It also refers to the auditory construction of the production including the actor's inflections and the application of sound effects and music. Composition involves the appreciation of emphasis, stability, and balance.

Emphasis

During each stage moment there must be at least one emphasis. This provides clarity for the audience who is perceiving the action for

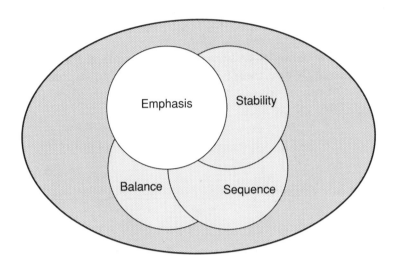

the first time. The basic method of obtaining emphasis is through a planned combination of body position, contrast, area, plane, level. **Body position** is the easiest way to maintain emphasis since full front commands attention. Center stage is the strongest area for emphasis especially in combination with the downstage plane. Whatever is higher than the regular line of vision onstage will receive emphasis through the use of level. **Contrast**, however, throws a completely different evaluation on the stage emphasis. An actor in a position different from the positions of the other actors will receive focus, even though the position may be considered weak. An actor with **space** around him or her will receive emphasis, but so will a figure with several figures closely behind it. For example, a character with two attendants draws focus more than a character with one attendant, as would a king with a large court than a rebel with a few followers.

Whenever actors look at a figure onstage or offstage, this visual focus creates direct focus. **Direct visual focus** is effective when using the configuration of a triangle in composition. **Triangles** can be used from scene to scene, or many triangles may be used in the same scene. This is one of the easiest ways to obtain direct focus while at the same time creating variety. Vary the size and the form of the triangle, or place triangles on the left and right sides of the stage rather than always center. Alter the base of the triangle in relation to the downstage edge. Add different levels, or create double triangles, or add figures to the legs of the triangle.

Using the Triangle for Direct Focus

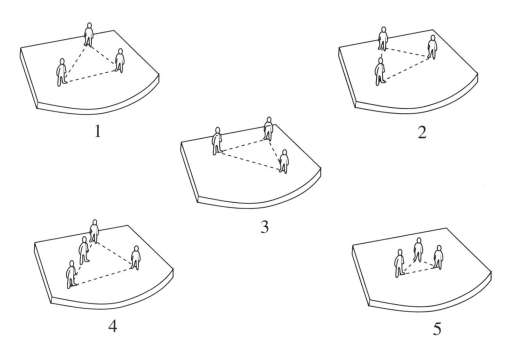

Counterfocus is also achieved when characters focus their attention on another character, activity, or object near them while in turn that character, activity, or object focuses on the main character being emphasized; indirect focus is accomplished.

These basic tools of emphasis can be further manipulated through three types of emphasis: double emphasis; secondary emphasis; and ensemble emphasis. **Double emphasis** employs the significance of two equally important figures. If there are more than two people onstage at the time of duoemphasis, it is best to block the others upstage center or midway between the two important figures. Although it may seem logical to block the others to one side of the stage, it is most undesirable. **Secondary emphasis** is given when an emphatic figure (direct focus) gives attention to another character, activity, or object.

Ensemble emphasis is needed when there are five or more principals on stage in an ensemble scene. Spread the figures roughly over the stage on the different pieces of furniture. Break the monotony of even spacing by having two sit on one sofa, another on the end of a desk, and so on. Be sure to avoid straight lines, but use many planes and areas. Have each actor take a different body position. In a composition such as this no one person is emphasized. Focus does not stop at any one figure but carries from one to another. The group should be so arranged that the eye, left to roam without the aid of sound, should go from one figure to another. Here, again, you have an opportunity to use many different methods of emphasis. Stretch your creativity.

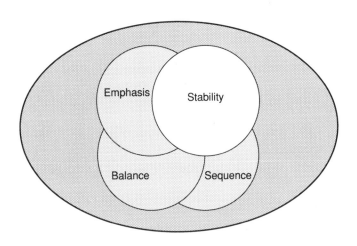

Stability

As a boat is tied to the dock to keep it from being damaged by currents or wind, so, too, a stage picture must be moored by weighting the composition with several figures. Stability is the element of composition that "anchors" the stage picture to the stage. It is achieved by blocking the weight of a character or group of characters in the downstage left and right corners. Occasionally a group lying downstage center can stabilize a larger group standing upstage. As the large group upstage increases in size, greater stabilizing weight is needed to strengthen the picture. Any broken line or diagonally straight line provides stability and emphasis. Again, it is better to avoid any straight lines except for special effect.

Stability

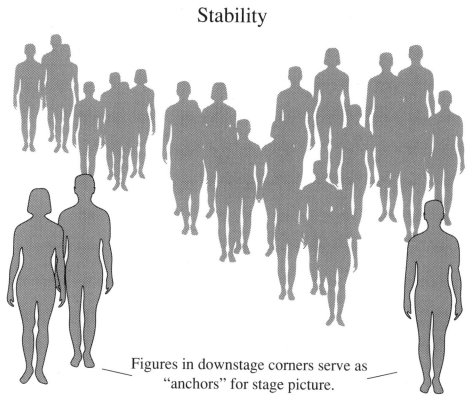

Figures in downstage corners serve as "anchors" for stage picture.

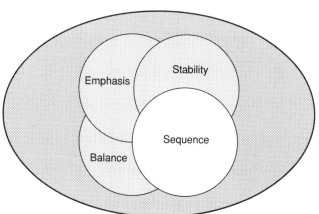

Sequence

A calculated progression of the distance between a single figure in relation to a small group and a crowd is called a sequence. Sequencing gives the illusion of a mass of people onstage. The single figure should be twice the distance from the small group that the small group is from the crowd.[3]

Sequence

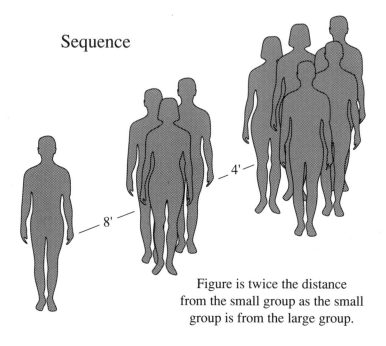

Figure is twice the distance
from the small group as the small
group is from the large group.

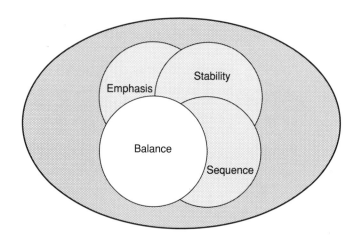

Physical Balance

Whenever you are dealing with two or more groups in two or more areas of the stage, you will need to consider balance. The physical balance of the stage composition can be either symmetrical or asymmetrical. Symmetrical balance obviously involves equal grouping of all elements that are equally spaced from an imaginary center line. Asymmetrical balance is the application of unequal numbers and unequal spacing.

Aesthetic Balance

It would be beneficial for you to know the fundamentals of the visual arts. Some of the essential ingredients in this subject are line, mass, and form. They produce an emotional response in the audience and comprise the most complex fundamentals for the beginning director to grasp.

Line is employed in a variety of ways to communicate emotional or tonal qualities in the play's action. Horizontal lines, with little mass, can create an undisturbed, quiet, tranquilizing, mechanical effect. Perpendicular lines can express aspiration, dignity, rigidity, grandeur— again depending on the weight of mass. Diagonal lines can be dynamic, forceful, eccentric, cutting, harsh. Straight lines convey strength, formality, regularity. Curved lines connote fluidity, flexibility, gracefulness, freedom. Broken lines have the effect of informality, disorder, individuality.

Mass refers to a group of characters in relation to a single character. In its basic rudiments, mass is the conception of lightness and heaviness in reference to characters grouped onstage. A greater number of figures positioned closely together relates a "heavy" feeling to the audience. On the other hand, fewer figures spread farther apart conveys a light effect. As you review the results of your analysis of the play, you will discover that each scene has an inherent weight, and the script will guide you in determining the configuration of mass. The resultant mass will convey to the audience the desired mood of the scene.

Form is necessary for scenes that include an ensemble of actors. Form can be either symmetrical or irregular, compact or diffused, shallow or deep. Regular or symmetrical form produces formality, hardness, calculation. Irregular form is more realistic, informal, unrestricted in its quality. Compact form suggests strength, power, energy, determination. Diffuse form creates the response of diversity, individuality, casualness, lack of discipline. Shallow form, within a single plane, induces artificiality, monotony, superficiality. Depth of form, more than one plane, expresses warmth, richness, a realistic effect.

Directors know that through all of this data there are no absolutes. Different combinations mean different things to different people. The information listed above is a collection of generalizations from which you can compose the composition of the stage picture. A variety of combinations of line, form, and mass may convey a mixture of contrasting moods to the audience. Contemporary realistic plays probably have broken line, irregular and deep form, and moderate mass—projecting the informal, individualistic, and scattered but reasonably substantial nature of modern life. Tragedies, or serious dramas, are likely to have fairly large mass, compact and regular form, and perpendicular lines—because of the strength, dignity, and formality of their environment and characters and the lofty nature of the issues involved. Comedies will tend toward curved and possibly broken lines (depending on how physical they are), delicate mass, and diffused or somewhat shallow form—which helps to communicate the sense of ease, freedom, fluidity, and positive, optimistic outlook on life that informs the comic sensibility.[4]

Balance

Line   Mass   Form

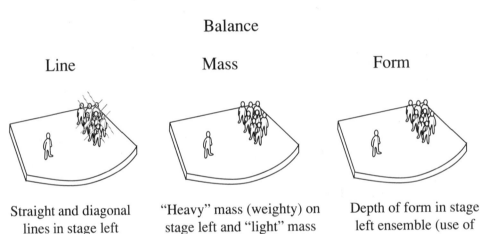

| Straight and diagonal lines in stage left ensemble. | "Heavy" mass (weighty) on stage left and "light" mass on stage right. Focus on single figure by use of space. | Depth of form in stage left ensemble (use of stage planes). Compact form of ensemble produces strength. |

Variety

All of the information offered so far should be generously applied with a spirit of variety. Variety, however, is a double-edged sword. Actors who aimlessly walk, sit, stand, and move about the stage for no reason other than the director told them to do so (merely in the interest of variety) will confuse and disappoint the audience. In fact, one of the marks of a poor director is the improper use of variety. The directorial purpose for every move on the stage is character motivation and textual clarity, with variety as a subordinate ingredient.

You may infuse variety in the areas described above through **body positions**. One or more actors may use all possible body positions in the course of the play, or as many different positions as possible in any one scene. Or you may find as many possible positions in a single **playing area**, e.g., around a chair, sofa, or table. The director's objective in seeking variety in **planes** maximizes the three-dimensional quality of the stage space. This technique is crucial for ensemble scenes and scenes involving two people. Find numerous possibilities for **levels** by exploring the endless possibilities of high and low.

Direct application of variety must be tempered with intelligence and logic. Variety is not a capricious manifestation of your authority. It is an inherent element in a play "creatively blocked to clarify the external action, to intensify the inner action, and to develop credibility, behavior, and the desired special effects—and if the play is a good one to begin with—it is difficult to conceive that the necessary variety will not be present."[5]

PICTURIZATION

Picturization is the concept whereby the techniques of composition are put to the test. The stage picture is a series of moment-to-moment snapshots in continuous evolution. Picturization is the freezing of any given moment in the play for the purpose of evaluating how powerfully and accurately the stage composition (without dialogue and movement) is representing the play's action. Here are the steps that will enable you to develop your picturization abilities.

First, as you begin to picture a scene (frequently bordered by the entrance and exit of a specific character, or perhaps the beats will mark the scene), review your conclusions when you analyze it. Give the **title** of the scene, its purpose, the objectives of the characters, and the attitudes of characters. Analyze each scene for purpose, character objectives, and attitudes so that it is given a title descriptive of its essence. This should be relatively easy after completing the extensive script analysis process outlined above.

Picturization
Step 1
Analysis and Title of Scene

Title of scene: Judas Returns Money

Purpose: To intensify the irreversibility
of the plot

Objectives: To expose hard hearts and
to relieve guilt

Attitudes: Extremes of resolve (Pharisees)
and desperation (Judas)

Second, determine the **emotional mood qualities** of the scene.
What kind of feeling is inherent in the action? Begin to think of the corresponding stage areas as shown below.

Picturization
Step 2
Possible Emotional Qualities of Stage Areas

UR	UC	UL
Sentimental	Majestic	Vastness
Amorous	Dominance	Mysterious
Gentle	Haughty	Melancholy
Imaginative	Judicial	Hopelessness
Remote	Formal	Otherworldly
DR	**DC**	**DL**
Casual	Bold	Reserved
Unpretentious	Strong	Soul-searching
Delicate	Resolute	Brooding
Gentle/Light	Mighty	Intrigue
Amiable	Climactic	Manipulative
Sincere		Business

Determining Mood Qualities

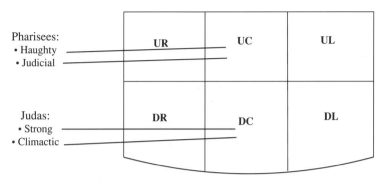

Refer to chart: Possible Emotional Qualities of Stage Areas

Third, think of the scene in terms of **line, mass, and form** as suggested above. Assign possible configurations based on the tonal quality of the scene. Refer to the descriptions above for these compositional elements. As an example, a scene of suspicion may have diffused mass, irregular line and form with diversified emphasis, uneven sequence and counterfocus with irregular body positions.

Picturization
Step 3
Expression of Step 2 in Line, Form, and Mass

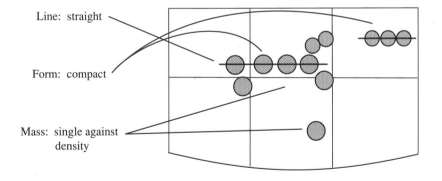

: actors that appear in this scene

Fourth, visualize the **scenic background** of the scene. Before you begin placing actors on the stage, you must clearly know where the set elements are located.

Picturization
Step 4
Visualize the Scenic Elements

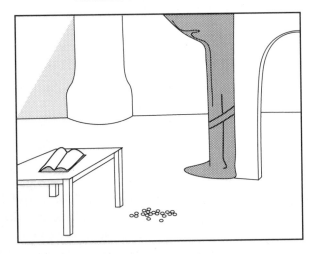

Fifth, begin to rehearse with the actors and **place** them according to the work you have completed so far. Try not to dictate the placement of each actor as much as work to discover your picture. Place the characters in roughly the proper areas of the stage according to the data collected thus far. The stronger the emotion of a scene, the more downstage it should be played. Social status, emotional stability of the char-

Picturization
Step 5
Actors Placed Without Gestures

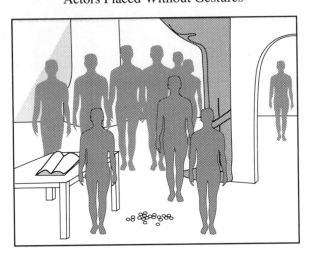

acters, and the course of action reveal numerous clues for the use of levels. Differing levels on the stage may mirror the increasing or diminishing emotional state of a character.

Finally, have the actors **add characterizations**, including the gestures of their characters, clearly indicating the emotional attitude of each character in relation to the action of the scene. Each actor must be creative with the picturization of individual characters.

Picturization
Step 6
Completed Stage Picture

All picturizations should contain subtleties and variety. Keep a checklist of how the tonal qualities of the areas and positions you have selected match the mood of the scene. Evaluate how the blocking reveals the relationships of the characters. In picturizations of deep emotional intensity or disorder and confusion, order and clarity must still be the hallmark of your stage picture.[6]

Several final suggestions for effective picturization include picturizing over and around obstacles. Encourage space separation between characters. Encourage actors to touch one another. Use gestures that best relay the emotional truth of the scene. Exploit gesture by taking actors to the fullest limits and then withdrawing them to the opposite extreme. Vary the continuous use of triangles. Encourage the use of hand properties that force varied body positions.[7] In review, here are the steps toward picturization:

STEPS TOWARD PICTURIZATION

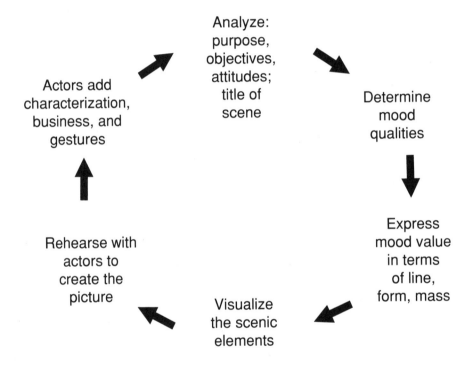

Analyze: purpose, objectives, attitudes; title of scene

Determine mood qualities

Actors add characterization, business, and gestures

Express mood value in terms of line, form, mass

Rehearse with actors to create the picture

Visualize the scenic elements

Picturizing and Blocking Crowd Scenes

Many directors begin with the visual impact of the play. Rather than responding to the first reading of a play with personal likes and dislikes, you may judge a play by whether it evokes images and seems to come alive in your imagination. This may make the visual impact of the play most clear and closest to the audience vision of the play. In the early stages of script research, search for one visual image that conveys the dramatic quality of the play. Reproduce this image by picturizing it onstage at the appropriate moment in the play's action. Sir Tyrone Guthrie, one of North America's greatest directors, said:

In all of my productions there is usually one central scene where I copied a picture. I didn't know how to do it, and I would look around for something that would give me a start on it. I didn't mind admitting that this was copied from that picture, because don't forget, the picture still has to move . . . So even if I start with a Rembrandt, I had to move the Rembrandt.[8]

Guthrie suggested that directors may find tremendous inspiration from the great masterpieces of Western art. Rembrandt, and many other masters of the canvas (Fernand Cormon, John Martin, Rubens, William Holman Hunt, Caravaggio, et al.) painted numerous biblical scenes, scenes involving very few figures, and scenes of great proportion. This is a great source from which to learn how to create beautiful stage pictures. Many professional directors use visual artworks, in addition to intense observation of life, to create compositions and picturizations of scenes in plays. Use the library or bookstore to uncover some great ideas for your picturization techniques.

One basic rule for making crowd scenes interesting also comes from director Tyrone Guthrie. It applies many compositional techniques at once: variety, gesture, area, body position, plane, levels. Since many Christian drama directors work with plays involving large ensembles or crowd scenes, this simple rule is most beneficial:

> To get maximum visual variety and emphasis in a scene with a large number of people but more than one focal point, tell the actors to focus on the action in several stages, but not to face the audience directly. Show them how an actor can contribute to the focus of the scene by first looking over the shoulder at the action, then, on a reaction, making a quarter turn; then perhaps, a little later, facing the action directly or turning to a partner nearby and exchanging glances or even leaning across the partner to whisper something to someone two persons away. Do not give every actor a specific move to make at a certain time, but allow the effect that can be achieved by each individual in the group finding a variety of positions in giving focus. There is nothing duller than seeing a crowd scene member moving back to the same position after a reaction. Make a point of telling people not to return to the same place after a reaction, to find a slightly different position in the same area.[9]

SIX

The Relationship of Dialogue to Movement

A play is not made up of disjointed picturizations. Each stage picture breathes life into the next one, and the next, and so on. Woven together, all picturizations flow seamlessly through a current of uncoiling emotions. The vehicle for these transitions from picture to picture is the movement. You become a master choreographer because you transform one-dimensional printing into three-dimensional actions. Everything you do should be well thought out and carefully planned. Organization and planning do not stifle creativity. On the contrary, creativity is facilitated by organization. You may be more spontaneous if you are well prepared.

MOVEMENT VALUES

There are basically three sources from which a director and an actor get ideas for movement: the playscript, the technical requirements, and the dramatic action in the subtext. Generally, movements can be classified in the categories of body movements, stage area movements, movements stage right to left, and diagonal movements, and contain varying degrees of strength and weakness:

The following body movements are considered **weak**:
- stepping backward
- slouching
- placing weight on the rear foot
- sitting down
- lowering the arm
- walking backward
- turning around and walking away from a figure

Or **strong** body movement:

- stepping forward
- straightening up
- placing the weight on the forward foot
- rising from a chair
- raising an arm
- walking forward

Relative strength of movement from **strong to weak**:
- any weak stage movement followed by a strong body movement will be a strong movement
- from any area to down center
- from up left or up right to any downstage area
- from up center to any downstage area
- from down left or right to any upstage area
- from down center to any other area
- any strong stage movement followed by a weak body movement will result in a weak movement[1]

The strength of a movement is obviously affected by **levels**. Moving to a higher level is strong unless punctuated by a weak body movement. The length of a movement also affects the tonal quality. Usually, walking a long distance will weaken the movement. If a movement is to be recognized as a legitimate movement, it should travel five feet or more. Shorter movements are stronger, but inexperienced actors tend to use nothing else, making the overall action choppy and lacking flow. Speed, intensity, and strength of the movement is determined by the character's emotional state and psychological condition.

The emotional impact of **entrances and exits** are related to the director's ground plan, the arrangement of physical objects (sets, furniture, props, steps, etc.). Upstage entrances are the strongest because they allow for the body position to be full front and the other actors to focus upstage. Strong exits are made downstage right since the exiting actor will be predominantly profile and will use a diagonal cross from up center. Some exits can be made stronger by having the character cross to the exit and deliver the exit line the moment before the exit. If overused, this can be melodramatic. Basically, exits are considered emphatic since they tend to give the tenor of the character at that moment.

The value of movements **from stage right to left** and stage left to right are influenced by the habits of Western civilization. Since the normal movement of the eye is from our left to right, a figure or group moving from the actor's stage left to right, contrary to our normal eye movement, gives a stronger effect. If a figure walks from our left across the stage to our right (stage right to left), this provides congruity. But if the figure passes from our right to left (stage left to right), this incongruity makes the figure appear stronger. Groups or characters who enter with a sense of strength should enter stage left, especially if the anticipation or the outcome is victory or success. If retreat or defeat is the intended mood, then the figure or group needs to move stage right to left.

The **tempo** of movement is dictated by the emotional state of each character. No two characters move at the same rate or tempo but according to the intensity of their intentions and objectives. An actor's understanding of his or her character's involvement in the dramatic action will determine the rate of movement for each acting moment.

Dialogue Values

Every line in a play has an inherent movement. Absolutely strong lines of dialogue must be used with strong movements. Absolutely weak lines must be used with weak movements. Mixed lines (strong and weak) demand correlating movements. Some lines receive their meaning from movement alone.

Generally speaking, actors should reserve movement to come **on the line**. Movement before a line emphasizes the line while movement after a line draws attention to the movement. **Pointing** the line is achieved by movement or action before the line such as:

- A pause in voice, business, or movement
- Taking an important position in a stronger area
- Contrast in vocal tone (e.g., full tone to whisper)
- Raising or lowering the pitch of the voice
- Using staccato on the important words
- Slowing down the tempo of the line[2]

Movement and Emphasis

The danger of movement is that the least amount of it may **pull focus**. While it is good for the beginning director to use as much movement as possible at first, and through subsequent rehearsals eliminate the excess movements, it is hazardous for any background figure to move during the focused dialogue of an emphatic character. Sometimes it is necessary to "freeze" a group or crowd scene during important dialogue.

Since movement is a visually powerful tool for emphasis, it is customary for actors to move during their own lines instead of during another's. Cues for movements during a line come from the dialogue itself. A line may explain, describe, or be expressive of a specific move. Entrance lines should be spoken during the entrance movements. Crosses made by speaking actors should be executed in front of a non-speaking actor. Exit speeches may be divided in half by the actor speaking a portion of his or her exit dialogue from one place, then after making the cross, delivering the remainder at the place of exit. The dialogue itself will dictate the manner and timing of the cross. Dialogue should not be held after someone exits. Otherwise, the action will seem disjointed and confusing.

MOVEMENT AND PICTURIZATION

As we have discussed, picturization is the visual storytelling of the play. If the picturization is true to the essence of the dramatic action, through the use of areas and variety, the playscript can be rendered without dialogue and for the most part still be understood by an audience.

Try to refrain from explaining with words to the actors' emotional states and character relationships. Rather, demonstrate through their movement and blocking the inner qualities of the characters and subtext of the play. As a general rule of thumb, you should strive to **show rather than tell**. This involves spacing the characters in accordance with their relationships, obtaining the correct body positions that convey the desired mood, and smoothly and accurately rendering transitions in movements as they reflect changes in relationships.

Movement **intensifies** the stage picture if the director increases the amount and size of movement. Methods of building a scene by movement alone include increasing the length of movement from shorter at the beginning to longer toward the end; increasing the number of people moving; using contrasting movements; going from weak body positions and levels to stronger ones; using stronger areas; and possibly increasing the number of people crossing one another.

Again, it is important that you approach your work with sound reason and logic. The picturization of scenes must evolve with **variety**.

Therefore, you will not want to apply the steps above to every scene in the play. Allow the dialogue to determine the mood and approach you will take toward a scene.

Contrasting movement, rather than parallel or countermovement, is to be encouraged. Parallel movement is two people moving identically in the same direction. Countermovement is two people moving identically in opposite directions. Use these for comedies, farces, or for special applications. Contrasting movement involves varying the activities of a figure or group.

There are basically four kinds of movement: (1) story movement, usually indicated by the playwright, necessary for the action to take place; (2) background movement, movement that establishes the atmosphere and location of a scene; (3) character movement, individual business that reflects the character's emotional state of mind; (4) and technical movement, movement that serves the compositional requirements of the stage picture for heightened picturization and transitional movements that seamlessly melt one stage picture into the next.

Movement may be thought of in terms of the laws of **kinetic energy**. Motion creates energy. When an actor moves he takes energy with him. When an actor leaves a place and heads to another place, he creates a "vacuum" in his wake. This vacuum needs to be filled, and another actor would logically fill in that vacuum. This is commonly called the **counter-cross.** You may think of the speed of the movement as its temperature. Thinking kinetically is even more important in arena and thrust staging. For instance, a straight line cross is stronger than a curved line cross in the proscenium stage, but curved crosses are essential actor movements for thrust and arena blocking.

Most importantly, every move onstage must have a **motivation**. Movement may be drawn from: (1) aesthetic motivation, the director's preplanned composition of intensely dramatic visual effects; (2) realistic motivation, the objective for which a movement is made (usually to complete a physical task); (3) psychological motivation, the character's thoughts and emotions; (4) character pattern motivation, the interplay of one character with another through successive scenes, actions, and reactions through picturization and movements that reveal the emotional and relational content of a scene and the subtext; (5) fundamental design motivation, the overriding movement that the director feels is the thematic thread of each composition.

Line, Form, and Mass

In our earlier discussion, the mood qualities of line, form, and mass were considered static. But line, form, and mass may move dynamically, either perpendicular (creating levels) or horizontal (across areas) or diagonal (traveling through planes). Tonal values of movements through levels, areas, and planes will remain consistent with the tonal values previously discussed. For instance, a heavy mass moving in one direction is powerful, while a diffused mass milling around results in turmoil, apathy, or instability.[3]

RHYTHM

Perhaps rhythm is the most difficult of all the fundamentals to teach to a director. For the modest scope of this book, it is impossible to give a thorough treatise on rhythm in drama. A mention of it may heighten your awareness of its dynamics.

There are basically two facets of rhythm in a play, **auditory** and **visual**. Rhythm is discovered by the playwright's patterning of speakers (indicating the broad rhythmic sweep of the play), the verbal strategy (repetition of words), the patterning of attitudes (specific rhythms of each scene), and the visual unfolding of events.

The first clue in determining the inherent rhythm of the script is the **kind of play** with which you are working. Comedies have lighter moods and quicker rhythms. Tragedies are heavier, perhaps slower. The nature of the situations in many of the scenes conveys a great deal about the play and its rhythm. Although the dialogue may be quite humorous, the situation may ultimately be tragic. The dialogue is a most obvious source of rhythm. The word choice of each character, the playwright's selection of the tonal vowels with their melodic contour, and the consonants with their percussive drive, give you clues as to the rhythmic nature of the play. Rhythm is to establish the mood of the play. A change in rhythm conveys a change in the mood of the scene. Perhaps it helps to think of rhythm in terms of pace and flow.

Pace is the audience's response to the actual duration of the scene. It can be fast or slow. A slow but controlled scene of emotional agony can engage the audience's attention for many minutes. A rapidly executed scene of comic chaos will seem timeless. Effective pacing engages the audience's concentration. Poor pacing does not.[4] Rhythm and pace are common to all of us (e.g., our heartbeat, the process of breathing). As a director, you may think of pacing elements of the play by monitoring:

1. Beats—between all beats there is rising action, climax, and resolution.
2. Dialogue—each line must give the exact meaning of the subtext.
3. Scenes—each scene must represent a continuity of the pace and flow of the play.
4. Actors—each must be within the rhythm of his or her character and situation.
5. Transitions—keep the tempo of movement and dialogue in harmony with the overall flow of the play.
6. Climax—make sure the pace becomes more dominant as emotional intensity increases.
7. Pauses—length is determined by the pace of dialogue, action, subtext, etc.
8. Entrances and exits—try to eliminate pauses unless called for in the action.
9. Laughter—build into the rhythm of the scenes pauses for audience laughter, otherwise actors will lose control of the builds.

The actor holding the stage from one scene to the next is the one who must maintain the pace and flow of the play, or reestablish the rhythm at the beginning of a scene with the entrance of a new character. Carry through the rhythm and reestablish it at the end of the scene.[5]

Acceleration of Tempo

This is perhaps the easiest of the tempo techniques to grasp. There are two facets of acceleration, the first of which is the "breaking up" of a scene. As an example let us divide a scene into four equal parts. The first quarter of the scene will be naturally interesting to the audience because of its newness. The second quarter may be accelerated by breaking up, which is making the movements shorter and increasing the speed of the delivery of the dialogue. The third quarter is broken up more than the second, and the fourth involves the fastest speed and the greatest number of people moving. Later scenes demand greater breaking up than earlier ones. The more dramatic action there is, however, the less need there is for acceleration.

Telescoping

Telescoping involves the quickening, or "picking up," of dialogue cues and movements from one character to the next, sometimes before the previous character has finished his or her line or movement. This is a more specific form of acceleration. It must be entered into gradually, for abrupt telescoping will be confusing. Actors of all levels should not have problems with this, although inexperienced ones may jump to it too quickly.

Tempos of Drop Scene

Again, we return to your analysis of the playscript. As we have seen through the development of this book, play analysis may be the most important process in the steps of a director's journey, and truly time demanding. Its rewards, however, are endless. Drop scenes, following climactic scenes, are approached by reversing the steps taken in building a scene. Drop scenes move from a scene of great intensity to a much lower level of intensity (strong emphasis on contrast).

Building the Play

At this point, check your analysis of the play by sensing the overall rhythm of the play as it builds from scene to scene. Review the play's structure and be able to think thoroughly about:

- Exposition
- Atmosphere and locale
- Establishment of mood and attitude
- Antecedent action revealing present and past relationships
- Main idea from which conflict will arise
- Lining up of forces
- Inciting factors
- Scenes that first suggest conflict
- The struggle
- The main conflict begins with rising action composed of minor climaxes alternating with transitional and drop scenes
- The climax
- The denouement

It is imperative to furnish the play with a progression of rhythms and tempos. The whole of the play should serve as a macrocosm of its many scenes. Each scene builds on the next as the entire play continually builds. For instance, in the play's forward movement, climaxes become longer in length and greater in intensity. Transitional scenes, drop scenes, and diminishing scenes (scenes of low emotional intensity) "become lower each time in proportion to the preceding climax, but actually they should never fall as low as at the beginning of the play. They also become shorter as the action of the play progresses."[6]

PART III

ACTORS AND ACTING

SEVEN

Basic Ingredients in Acting Techniques

To this point, you are aware that the process of play production involves speculating about a play, planning the work, creating the designs, and consolidating all of the details. As a result of your research period, the play has been analyzed and the visual composition begins to take shape. Actors, which you selected from auditions and/or interviews, have been assigned to their characters. Now you will approach the actors with a visual concept of how the play should look. Through the course of rehearsals, you will work with actors to transform your visual concept into movements that clarify the play's action. Getting the most out of the actor's voice and movements is your constant challenge every moment of every rehearsal. Let's turn to the director's technique of unleashing the actor's creative potential.

The best way for you to use this chapter is to appropriately combine the concepts and exercises with the natural flow of your rehearsals. Few church drama directors have the luxury of actor training sessions apart from work on a specific play. For this reason, incorporate obtainable elements of actor training concepts and activities into the rehearsal plan as they apply directly to the action in the script. Each element of acting training will be followed by a series of exercises useful during the rehearsal period or for classroom sessions.

The Oxford Companion to the Theatre states that an actor should be a "singer, dancer, mimic, acrobat, tragedian, comedian—and to have at his command a good physique, a retentive memory, an alert brain, a clear, resonant voice with good articulation and controlled breathing." To this end, the essential components of acting will be listed, followed by an exercise to awaken this quality within an actor. Group discussion and evaluation are essential conclusions to any actor training exercise.

Relaxation

It would be prudent to begin every rehearsal with a few minutes of physical and vocal warm-ups to prepare the actor's instrument for the demands of interpreting a role. Begin with a relaxation exercise.

Each actor lies on his back. Concentrate on regular, low breathing. Imagine each body cell melting into the floor. Take a low breath and release on a long hissing "ss." Pause for regular breathing. Take a low breath and release on a buzzing "zz," feeling the vibrations between the front teeth, keeping the jaw relaxed. Now isolate each part of the body (foot, ankle, calf, etc.) and concentrate tension on that specific part. After that part is shivering with tension, quickly release all tension. The actor should concentrate on how relaxed that part of the body has become after applying and then releasing tension.

Or a more simple version would begin with each actor sitting in a chair like a "rag doll," head bowed and arms hanging to the side. Concentrate on relaxing each part of the body. After one minute, bring the neck and head to an erect position.

Concentration

The foundation upon which the creativeness of an actor rests is concentration. Good actors focus all of their attention on the character and environment of the play at all times. Attention diverted to the auditorium or audience, or self-consciousness, or anything that draws the attention of the actors away from the reality of the characters and the world onstage confirms a lack of concentration. Creativity is nourished by actors whose very nature is one of concentration. A lack of concentration diffuses energy and dilutes the creative actions of the actors.

Working individually, each actor will concentrate on reproducing the sensory experience of drinking a cup of coffee. The director will challenge the actors by verbally drawing attention to specific details (e.g., smell, temperature on tongue, space between fingers for the handle). This exercise is the precursor of sensory memory exercises used later.

Observation

Preparation as an actor and constructing a character onstage require intense observation of people, situations, and life itself. Ask that the actors begin keeping a written journal, entering daily observations of their life and the world around them.

Have each actor go to the zoo and compose a written observation of an animal of his or her choice. During acting sessions, each actor will meticulously reproduce the exact physical qualities and rhythm of the animal.[1]

Imagination

By developing concentration and observation you are also developing the imagination. Truly creative processes begin with the imagination. Intense observation of the life and world of an actor and his or her powers of concentration are the products of the right life of his or her imagination.

One actor begins a motion accompanied by a sound as the first ingredient to building a machine. As the other actors are inclined, each one joins in with his or her own imagined movement and sound until the entire cast is involved. (The director may want to have a video camera nearby because this exercise frequently produces creative and humorous results.)

Sensory Memory

Many aspects of actor training dovetail into one another. Through the powers of concentration, the actor seeks to strengthen his or her imagination and observation. The senses provide abundant resources for such activity.

Developing sensory memory is an application of observation, concentration, and imagination. In a daily journal, the actor records observations that are in turn reproduced by concentrating on details ignited by the imagination. Sensory memory is a technique whereby the actor channels energy away from self-consciousness and into aspects of acting described above. It is another step to building a character.

Reproduce with great detail drinking a cup of coffee, smelling an odor, eating food, shaving, or pantomiming a location. Begin with one sensory experience. As the actors become more adept, add two and then three sensory elements to an exercise. Move from specific sensory exercises, like the coffee cup, to complete bodily sensations such as water or an imagined climate. Add sensory elements to improvised scenes. Combine any sensory exercise with any other acting exercise.

Emotional Memory

Portraying emotions is a large part of the actor's task. Exploration into an actor's facility of emotional portrayal becomes an essential ingredient in training an actor.

Recalling emotional experiences in an actor's life facilitates the actor in portraying emotions within the construct of a character. This technique is frequently used as "substitution" for which an actor recalls an emotional experience from his or her own life similar to the situation of the character he or she is portraying. The actor seeks deeper understanding of the character from this mutual approach to emotions.

Ask the actors to re-create an emotional experience from their own life that is similar to an emotional experience of the character they are portraying. Encourage them to transfer their acting exercise experience to the reality of their character's scenes.

Inner Action

It is most logical at this point for the actor to become aware of inner action. Verbalizing emotions or commenting on sensory experience is usually preceded by an inner action. All of us have watched the actor who has just commented on the heat and then pantomimed wiping sweat from his brow. Inner action reverses such action. A character realizes within himself that he is hot. Then he silently observes that he is sweating. The character wipes the sweat from his brow. As a result of this gesture, which began as an inner action, a line is spoken. Inner action usually precedes an activity or dialogue.

The actors are invited to a mansion for a dinner party. During appetizers, the host comes over a public address system and announces that he will soon pass away and each guest will inherit $1 million.

The actors are a group of refugees ready to leave on a helicopter. The helicopter, however, holds three less than the number of actors participating.

Inner and Outer Tempos

It is important for an actor to understand that the human body is governed by two rhythms, one dependent on the character's internal emotional influences and the other on external environmental influences. A character may experience quick changes in thought while executing a slow action or speech.

Have the actors apply the rhythms observed in the animal at the zoo to a character in an improvised scene. The inner tempo of the animal should contrast the external tempo of the improvised scene.

Imaginary Body

In portraying a character in a play it is necessary to be at least familiar with the imagined physical attributes of the character. Many of the exercises previously noted help an actor create a variety of rhythms, tempos, and physical movement. As these aspects come together, an actor can portray the imagined physical posture and movements of a character.

Observe a personal characteristic of someone else (manner of walking, eyes, mouth, etc.). Re-create this using your own body.

Solicit ideas from the cast about various physical postures and their emotional connotations. Have the actors improvise short scenes incorporating these ideas. Discuss how re-creating an imaginary body produces emotional feelings.[2]

▶▶▶ EIGHT ◀◀◀

Working with the Actor's Voice

The actor's voice and approach to constructing a character on the stage are deeply related to the text of the script. As it is appropriate to begin with physical warm-ups before each rehearsal, it is equally essential that the actors begin with vocal warm-ups.

Before a list of vocal warm-ups is offered, it is necessary to be familiar with the process of vocal production. Basically, there are four areas of vocal production: breathing, phonation, articulation, and resonance (for the technique of singing the categories are expanded).

Breathing

Good posture is the first essential of good breathing. Although there is no one perfect posture for all people, the image of a marionette hanging from one string attached to the top of the head and another to the breastbone is a creative beginning. If the head is erect and the chest is lifted, then the pelvis should "hang" naturally in place.

There are three types of breathing: chest, rib, and abdominal (or diaphragmatic). Chest breathing (clavicular breathing) is highly discouraged.

Rib breathing is effected by the conscious use of the external intercostal muscles (running diagonally from the backbone down the ribs), which are used for inhalation and the inner intercostals (running diagonally from the backbone up the ribs) for exhalation. Lifting the back lower section of the ribs for inhalation increases breathing efficiency.

The most important breathing muscle is the **diaphragm**, a large dome-shaped muscle dividing the chamber of the heart and lungs from the digestive area. Expansion of the abdominal muscles draws the diaphragm downward for inhalation. Control of these muscles, while the lower back ribs remain raised and suspended, provides a longer breath flow for exhalation. In 20th-century fashion trend, the

110

flat, firm stomach image may inhibit many actors from diaphragmatic breathing. *Efficient breathing is a combination of abdominal and rib breathing and is the key to vocal projection.*

Phonation

As breath passes through the larynx, its flow is controlled by a lower set of vocal folds (unfortunately referred to as "cords") and an upper set of vocal tissues. The lower pair vibrate and produce sound. This operation is called "phonation." The upper set seldom produce sound. They are used to help close the larynx or to assist the lower folds during the execution of a stage whisper. Above these tissues is the epiglottis, which closes the larynx completely to prevent a foreign body from entering or for swallowing.

The most efficient balance between the tension in the vocal tissues and the contraction of the breathing muscles is the aim of phonation and is called a **good attack**. An imbalance results in either breathiness or tightness.

Articulation

As the breath, now in the form of pitch vibration, leaves the larynx, it enters the oral cavity and is manipulated into speech. Articulation is the formation of words through the proper execution of vowels, diphthongs, and consonants. The essentials of good diction include enunciation and pronunciation. Correct breathing and efficient phonation provide the bedrock of articulation. Tension in the oral cavity is an actor's enemy. Articulation is the key to clarity and expressiveness.

Resonance

Resonance is as complex as the other areas and equally important. Simply put, resonance is the application of the science of acoustics whereby a complex configuration of frequencies produced naturally by the vocal process greatly determines the tonal quality and intensity of the voice. The cavities of air above the larynx are the resonating chambers. Singers and actors learn to think about "shaping" the tissues, membranes, and spaces above the larynx (combined with improved diction and breathing) to enhance resonation.

Vivid mental images of placement of the voice and intense concentration on lifting the soft palate, relaxing the tongue, opening the throat, lowering the larynx (but not forcing it lower), and loosening the jaw constitute a lifetime of study for many actors and singers in the effort of improving resonance. Essentials of good resonance include a combination of the extremes of brilliance and depth. Resonance adds richness and dimension to the actor's voice. Any exercises utilizing humming in the front of the face are excellent for resonance.

VOCAL WARM-UPS

Neck, Head, Shoulders, and Spine

- Roll the head slowly down, to the left, to the back, to the right and reverse. Always keep the jaw relaxed.
- Lift the shoulders as high as they will go and hold them there. Then suddenly drop them into a relaxed position. Repeat.
- Roll the shoulders forward and backward.
- Massage the facial muscles.
- Vigorously shake the arms.
- Begin to "feel the weight of the head dragging on the spine, gradually giving in to the weight so that the spine undoes, giving in to gravity, vertebra by vertebra, from the top down. Try to picture the vertebra one by one. Let your knees relax so that the weight remains over the middle of the feet. Check that your weight does not rock back on your heels or forward on your toes. Check that your knees do not lock. When the weight is too much to support through balance, release the spine quickly and hang upside down. Imagine your torso is hanging from your tailbone, giving in to the force of gravity. Breathe easily. You are doing this to relax all the torso muscles, shoulder muscles, neck muscles, head and arms. Now focus your attention on your tailbone and, from there, begin to build the spine up again, vertebra by vertebra, as though building a castle of nursery bricks one on top of the other. Do not use the stomach muscles; leave them hanging loose; breathe. Do not suddenly straighten the knees; let them gradually straighten as the balance shifts. Find the vertebrae that lift the rib cage, and build them up from the small of the back. You are now an upright, headless torso. Focus on the top seven vertebrae that make up the neck, and gradually build

them up on top of the rest of the spine. Be aware that the head floats up as a result of the neck build. You do not 'lift your head.'" Keep lengthening and widening throughout. Pause and repeat once.[1]

Lips, Tongue, and Jaw

- Lightly and rapidly:
    "wee-wee-wee-wee-wee-wee-wee-wee-wee"
    "waw-waw-waw-waw-waw-waw-waw-waw"
    "wee-waw-wee-waw-wee-waw-wee-waw-wee-waw"

- With the jaw relaxed, point the tip of the tongue straight out, then in, and repeat. Do the same with right to left and repeat. Then combine out-in-right-left.

- Alternate repeating the following phrases:
    paper poppy
    baby bubble

- Repeat each phrase three times as fast as possible:
    "Can't you, won't you, don't you" (Do not say "can-chew")
    "Did you, would you, could you" (Do not say "could-jew")

- Repeat each of the following phrases as rapidly as possible:
    "topeka, topeka, topeka, topeka . . ."
    "mommala, poppala, mommala, poppala . . ."

- Leave the teeth open, the tongue relaxed, and the jaw uninvolved. Open and close the lips, increasing in speed. Now bring the lower lip to touch the upper lip and visa versa.

Resonance

- Repeat the following phrases slowly, concentrating on the breath flow and the "m," "n," and "ng" in each word so that the vibration of the hum is felt in the lips, nose, and forehead (frequently referred to as the mask):
    "Many men making much money."
    "Many men, many men, many men, men, men, men, men."
    "Miles and miles of golden smiles."
    "One by one by one they come."
    "The murmuring of doves in immemorial elms."
    "Five miles meandering with a mazy motion."
    "Going, going, going, gone."

Stress

- Do the "traveling stress" exercise, speaking five times each the one-to-five sequence or the sentences below, strongly and clearly emphasizing the next number or word on each repetition as shown in the first sequence. Be sure that the voice is firm, easy, and fully supported when you speak the stressed number or word, and that it does not feel tense or sound strained. The sentences below contain most of the vowel and diphthong sounds of American English in the usual groupings.

  1. <u>one</u>, two, three, four, five
     one, <u>two</u>, three, four, five
     one, two, <u>three</u>, four, five
     one, two, three, <u>four</u>, five
     one, two, three, four, <u>five</u>

  2. I will not go there.

  3. You must tell her soon.

  4. He thinks four should wait.

  5. Call me if you hear.

  6. Now your plans are spoiled.

  7. We will spend cash.

  8. You should call Tom.

  9. Take my boy home now.

  10. Your chores are shared here.

- Do the "picketies" exercise, counting aloud from one to five, speaking clearly and firmly and saying the nonsense word "pickety" as three unstressed syllables between numbers. Speak the "pickety" crisply, being careful not to slur, swallow, or merely to make a pitch change pattern of high for the number and low of the "pickety."

  <u>One</u> pickety, <u>two</u> pickety, <u>three</u> pickety, <u>four</u> pickety, <u>five</u>.

- Other traveling stress exercises:

  <u>One</u> into a <u>two</u> had to be <u>three</u> went for a <u>four</u> was in my <u>five</u>.

  <u>Try</u> to <u>take</u> the <u>time</u> to <u>choose</u> the <u>best</u>.

  <u>Make</u> them <u>ask</u> the <u>judge</u> to <u>hear</u> your <u>plea</u>.

  <u>Tom</u> will <u>know</u> the <u>score</u> and <u>he</u> can <u>tell</u> us.

  <u>All</u> the <u>plates</u> were <u>scratched</u> or <u>chipped</u> or <u>broken</u>.

Shouting

- Since shouting is the result of strong emotional involvement, it must be approached gradually within the context of the emotion. First, produce the sound with an open throat and mouth but not yet yelling. Now imagine the scene that produces the emotion. Use just a few words to express the emotion. Repeat the scene several times, each time becoming louder. Constantly monitor yourself for tension in the shoulders, neck, and throat. Allow the emotional content of the scene to prepare your body for proper shouting. Continue to develop diaphragmatic breathing. Always "feel" the shout low in your body rather than high in your throat.

DICTION

Early in the 20th century, Richard Boleslavsky, a prodigy of Constantin Stanislavski, asked the man who was the model for George Bernard Shaw's character of Henry Higgins in *Pygmalion* to teach his cast members how to speak with an Irish accent. Upon completion of the training, Boleslavsky asked why the cast could not learn their own language as well as they had learned the Irish dialect. From that point on, good American speech has been taught in schools of theatre, with the curriculum centering on seven key points. Here are three of those seven principles for accurate American theatre speech:

1. The "Long U"

The "long U" is composed of the consonant "y" (as in "yak") and the vowel "oo" (as in "you") when following the sounds "t," "d," and "n," as in: tune, tutor, opportunity, gratitude, due, dew, endure, adieu, dualist, new, ingenuity, neutral, renew, lute, resolution, salute, concludes, consume, pursue.

2. Ending Consonants T, D, and L with You and Your

A common mispronunciation of "can't you" is "can't chew," or "did you" as "didjew," or "will you" with the tongue giving it a swallowed sound. These are to be avoided. Enunciate the "t" and "d" distinctly from the "you" or "your" that follows. For the double "l," the tip of the tongue has to be raised behind the upper front teeth and then relaxed behind the lower teeth for "you."

3. The Voiceless Consonant

Use the voiceless consonant "wh" involving a strong stream of breath in such words as "which," "why," "whine," and "where."[2]

NINE

Characterization

Once again we arrive at a topic that cannot be treated adequately in a few pages. Character analysis begins with the script analysis for both the director and the actor. While it is not the director's job to portray a character onstage, you should know how to guide others to do it and do it well.

As you rehearse a scene, you need to know how to diagnose the actor's work and offer an effective and quick remedy. Most directors carefully guide actors through the blocking and review stages of the rehearsal process by interjecting directions as needed. But once you begin polishing, you need to sit back and take notes. **Do not interrupt the flow of the actors work while they are in a polishing or run-through phase, unless absolutely necessary.** Take notes. At the conclusion of the scene or rehearsal, gather the cast on the stage and read through your notes. (They should write your suggestions in their script with the pencil they bring to every rehearsal.) Help actors in the development of their characterization. Below are a few thoughts you my want your actors to be aware of.

From the experiences of the various exercises above, the actors stock a toolbox from which they can **externalize the internal aspects** of a character. In the entire process observation and imagination provide the foundation for characterization. Each actor must formulate what the character is thinking and feeling while onstage and offstage. The actor must determine a motive for each moment of the character's existence.

Every portrayal must have **energy** so that the actor's created life on the stage is sustained. Energy is the concentrated channeling of energy during the rehearsal period and performance. Energy is not to be confused with loudness or exaggeration. Again, the objective is clarity. Energy is the urgent manifestation of everything a character needs to communicate to other characters.

Constant repetition of the same vocal inflection and physical gesture diminish the impact of the actor's work. Therefore, an actor must instill **variety** into the portrayal. As mentioned earlier, variety for the sake of variety is not necessarily the best approach. Rather, variety is a logical, creative, and intellectually justifiable series of choices that brush a characterization with strokes of imagination. This is one of the purposes of stage business.

Whenever an actor portrays a character onstage, the actor must believe in everything the character says and does at the moment he or she speaks or acts. This wholehearted concentration provides **truth** to the characterization. Whenever a line is spoken or a move is executed, the actor performs them with honesty and commitment, ideally devoid of self-conscious monitoring of how well the audience likes the actor's portrayal. Stage business reinforces the truthfulness of a character. If an actor's business is inconsistent with the rest of the characterization, then the truth of the character has been fractured. On the other hand, if all of the characterization is consistent and engaging, it is truthful.

You may find it necessary for actors to **improvise** the events that take place before the play begins, or events that may occur after the play ends, or events that take place offstage between scenes. This will assist the actors in grasping more thoroughly a rationale for their characters' stage business, their contribution to the play's actions, and their relationships with other characters. An excellent exercise to this effect is detailed in appendix A of Stanislavski's *Preparing a Role*. For a definitive treatment of characterization in the modern realism genre, commonly referred to as the "method," consult Stanislavski's final installment of his actor training triptych, *Building a Character*.

DIAGNOSTIC QUESTIONS FOR CHARACTERIZATION

An actor may use the following diagnostic questions to formulate a characterization:

1. What is the basic or central idea set forth in the play?

2. How does your character contribute to the central idea of the play?

3. Is your character honestly drawn, or has he or she been distorted in order to affect the overall intent of the play?

4. Indicate several illustrations of action and dialogue of your character that help to reveal the thematic idea of the play.

5. How does the style of the play affect the manner and movement in which your character should be performed?

6. How do the factors of age, social status, dress, education, occupation, health, physical environment, climate, and familiarity with surroundings suggest the type of movement to be used in the portrayal? Will any of these factors necessarily change your normal speaking voice?

7. How do the mood of the play and the costumes affect the movement to be used in the portrayal?

8. Does the playwright indicate any necessary movement or business that must be incorporated into the character? If so, what does it suggest about playing the role?

9. Are there any critical pieces of furniture or props that will affect movement and business? Can they be used to sharpen your character?

10. What is the main motivation of your character in the play?

11. What significant comments does the character make about himself or herself that reveal aspects of the characterization?

12. What significant comments are made about your character by other characters in the play?

13. What does the playwright say about your character in the notes?

14. What obstacles exist that prevent your character from achieving his or her goals?

15. How does your character deal with the obstacles that confront him or her?

16. Are there differences in language from one character to another that tend to clarify characterizations?

17. Is your character's dialogue dissimilar to that of the other characters? What does it reveal about your particular character?

18. In what ways are you and your character similar? Different? Explain how you can portray both in the action of the play.

19. Does your character speak with any dialect or use particular regionalisms in his or her speech? Explain.

20. What selections of clothing and music ultimately describe your character?

21. What vocal, physical, and acting exercises will you consistently maintain in order to create your character?[1]

To organize all the information you have gathered, make a checklist for the character by compiling the data into the following categories:

Sentence Structure: How does the character talk?

Vocabulary: Why does the character choose certain words?

Allusion: Why does the character speak allusions?

Formality: Why is the character formal or informal?

Topics: What does the character talk about and why?

Tone: What emotional tone pervades the character's actions?

Complexity: What makes the character complex?

Personal Relationships: How does this explain the character?

Perception: What are the perceptions of the character?

Philosophy: How does the character relate this?

Suppression: Why does the character engage this?[2]

Construct a personal history of the character that includes all the known incidents in the character's life. Write a cultural history of the character from the study of his or her actual culture, the playwright's culture, or the culture constructed in the playwright's imagination, depending on what setting the playwright chose.

Have the cast members complete a handout on character analysis like the one below. Or, compose one of your own with more detailed questions.

Character Analysis

Analysis

1. "Who am I?" Search for the character's life prior to the play's beginning. Compose a biography including family background, environment, etc.

2. What is the function of the character in the play? How does the character move forward the dramatic action of the play?

3. What characteristics or traits are most important?

4. List all the adjectives you can think of to describe the character.

Physical Characteristics

Age

Race

Body type and carriage

Strength

Health

Movements

Speech

Dress

Mental Characteristics

Native intelligence

Thinking habits

Education

Originality

Personal Characteristics

Basic attitudes: likes, dislikes toward life, toward other characters in the play

Ways of meeting a crisis, conflict, or change in environment

Capacity for deep feeling

Stability

Self-control

Temperament: genial, domineering, etc.

Social Characteristics

Profession: daily routine

Nationality

Religion

Social class

Economic status

Symbols Suggesting Human Qualities

Animal

Machinery

Objects

Scenes

"What do I want in this scene?" (objective)
"What do I do to get what I want?" (action)
"What is in my way?" (obstacle)

What essence in the character will help him or her get it?
What essence in the character will prevent him or her from getting what he or she wants?
Where is the climax of highest point of action for your character?

TEN

Pathology of Bad Acting

Here are 20 common signs of less than professional acting and some suggested remedies, which can be used while the actors are in rehearsal.

1. Bending at the waist toward the person spoken to.

Amateur actors tend to bend at the waist toward the person to whom they are speaking. This stems from a physical sense that our voices and words are not getting the meaning across. So our bodies "kick in" extra movements for emphasis. What usually results is that both the dialogue and physical presence of the actor are weakened. For these actors, physical warm-ups are essential. Continue to remind the entire cast to let the words and voice do the work. Trust the text to convey the strength of its meaning and work on relaxing the body. Have the actors go through each scene to discover how many movements are not clearly motivated.

2. Shrugging of shoulders.

Frequently actors who need to respond to something in a scene where no response is specified will look at the audience and shrug their shoulders. This is a weak choice and should only be used when it is clearly needed to communicate an idea. Otherwise, encourage actors to make strong choices based on the action in the scene.

3. Nonuse of hands above the waist.

Many amateur actors refrain from using their hands above the waistline. Instruct the actors that the weakest area of expression in the hands and arms is below the waistline. The stronger area of expression for the arms and hands lies between the waistline and the top of the

123

shoulders. The strongest field of expression for gestures occurs when the hands and arms are raised about the shoulders. Have actors analyze the emotional content of a scene and apply these principles to the character's gestures.

4. Not knowing what to do with hands.

Amateur actors do not always know what to do with their hands. Give this actor a hand prop that can become a part of the actor's stage business. Give him or her a costume with pockets. Use a shoe or a block of wood and have the actor pass the object to the actor to whom he or she is talking. Have the actor throw a "lightning bolt" to the actor with whom he or she is speaking.

5. Creating no theatre business (gesture and movement).

Many actors have problems creating gestures and movements onstage. Have them improvise in the environment of the scene, interacting with everything they "see" in the scene. Have the actors do a separate improvisation in which they must do an activity in an environment of their choice, recreating the life of the scene with great detail. Have the actors rehearse with "silent dialogue," going through the scene as though they are speaking their lines but do not. The scene must be filled with only the physical interpretation of the lines.

6. Having fear of touching others or being touched.

Some inexperienced actors have a fear of physical contact during their scenes. Pair the actors and do the mirror exercise. Or as the pair of actors are facing one another, both close their eyes as one gently explores the face of the other with his or her hands.

7. Moving aimlessly about the stage.

Some actors move without purpose through a scene. Teach actors that all movement must be motivated. Discuss the beats of the scene and the character's objectives. Determine how specific movements at specific times in the dialogue interpret the text. Actors without lines must decide what it is they are doing or thinking at every moment. Encourage them to be creative!

8. Feeling they must sit down on stage.

Other actors feel they must sit down as often as possible. For one rehearsal, remove the furniture. Do any exercise that encourages physical interpretation.

9. Shifting weight back and forth.

Amateur actors invariably shift their weight back and forth on their feet while in dialogue. Simply reiterate as often as necessary to "stop shifting your weight back and forth." If necessary, have an actor play an entire scene in one place while you physically hold down their shoes with your hands.

10. Never listening to other actors.

Sometimes it is difficult for inexperienced actors to truly listen to other actors. Do an exercise where one actor tries to talk another into doing something. Then apply the same kind of energy to a scene in the play. Or run a scene in the play where the other actors paraphrase their lines to the actor who tends not to listen. Or have actors temporarily exchange parts.

11. Emoting rather than relating with fellow actors.

Amateur actors frequently give too much "acting" as they speak rather than simply talk to fellow actors. The result is an exaggerated, unnatural delivery, sometimes even melodramatic. Do exercises in sensory memory, or have the actors whisper their lines.

12. Reading lines mechanically.

Others will read lines mechanically. Have these actors sing their lines during a rehearsal. Encourage traveling stress exercises and a generous portion of vocal warm-ups. (See chapter eight.)

13. Poorly enunciating and rushing lines.

Many actors have poor enunciation and rush quickly through their lines. Vocal warm-ups and diction exercises are absolutely essential for all rehearsals. Concentrate on the emotional qualities of the vowels and consonants in relation to the emotional qualities of the scene. Have the actors say their lines in slow motion. Constantly and politely remind everyone to slow down until it becomes habitual.

14. Repeating a line they misread.

Some actors habitually repeat a line when they make a mistake. Encourage word-for-word memorization, but eventually enable them to improvise with misread lines. "When you misread a line, go with it. Please do not repeat it."

15. Mouthing other lines.

Some actors continually mouth the lines of the other actors in order to keep their place. Compliment them on their fine memorization skills and refer to number 10.

16. Casting eyes downward.

If actors continually cast their eyes downward, have them use a flashlight in a scene. Darken the rehearsal room. The actors with the flashlight must use it as their eyes, shining it in the face of anyone to whom they are speaking or looking. Then remove the flashlights, turn on the lights, and encourage the actors to re-create the same kind of "eye-focus."

17. Having no feeling for characterization.

Most amateurs have little feeling for the characterization of their portrayal. The animal exercise as mentioned earlier proves most helpful. Encourage the actors to keep a character scrapbook and/or rehearsal journal in which all ideas and thoughts about the character are recorded. This may include clippings, photographs, research information, observations, and reflections on the character being portrayed. Have actors interviewed in character by the other characters in the play. Ask the actors to write a complete biography of their character. Make sure actors know the answers to many of the questions brought up in chapter nine.

18. Hanging on to props and furniture.

Actors who like to hang on to props or furniture need to have the furniture or props removed for several rehearsals while transferring the energy of their interpretation to physical gestures and business. Also see the remedies suggested for number 4.

19. Failing to project emotions or voice.

Many untrained actors do not project their voice or their emotions. This is another reason why physical, vocal, and imagination warm-ups at the beginning of rehearsals are so essential. They help prepare the actor's instrument for the demands of acting. For people who do not project, take them through a series of breathing exercises to awaken the diaphragm. Stress the need to take low and generous breaths throughout a scene and then "share their voice" with the back row.

To increase the projection of emotions, use coaching phrases like "Expand that" while the actors are working, or add silence to heighten the moment of emotional intensity.

20. Lacking emotional development in fingers.

A lack of energy in the arms and hands usually results in a lack of energy in the fingers. Although seemingly insignificant, fingers are a powerful source of physical portrayal. Ask actors to rehearse scenes with no dialogue, but communicate the action and their characterization with just their hands and fingers. Again, many of the exercises previously mentioned (e.g., animal observation) can be modified or expanded to remedy a variety of situations. Or create exercises of your own, based on the text or action in the play to help actors find the truth in their portrayal.

There are hundreds of books written about the art of acting. Encourage actors to study their craft by taking acting classes, reading, going to plays, and observing the technique of fine stage actors. As the director, you may also want to take an acting class in order to teach one in your church in between productions. Most universities and community colleges offer actor training for adults. Attend workshops and conferences that you know offer practical training for the director and actor. Above all, treat your actors with the utmost respect and reward their commitment and hard work with generous and earnest praise.

PART IV

TECHNICAL PRODUCTION

ELEVEN

Constructing the Set Design

"Less Is More"

Our goals are to learn, to teach, to move others, and to communicate truth. Our activities include the principles of aesthetics, and many churches need to rediscover aesthetic thinking. Theatre in the church is a valid path to that end, but scenic design and set construction in the church do not have to be so elaborate as to re-create reality. Theatre is the illusion of reality, not reality itself. The subtle use of simple scenic pieces and set properties accomplishes more in the imagination of an audience than thousands of dollars spent on detailed set construction. This is not to impugn aesthetic pursuits in scene design. On the contrary, Christians should continue to appreciate on deeper levels the concepts of beauty, order, balance, color, and arrangement.

A well-written playscript and fine actors will stimulate the imaginations and hearts of Christians more fully than an expensive set without the former. Yet we cannot ignore that the essential elements of technical production in the 21st-century church involve lighting, sound, and costumes. The construction of large auditoriums forces us to equip the facility appropriately, or seek a smaller assembly hall where sound reinforcement is not needed and a few lighting sources are sufficient. If Christian theatre is to operate in large halls, then adequate lighting, brilliant costumes, and professional sound equipment must be employed. Consequently, financial commitments should be channeled to these areas.

Practically speaking, many churches simply do not have the resources from which to draw for such expensive items as lighting, sound, and costumes. Therefore, when considering scene design, create from the idea that "less is more." Construct scenery that suggests, rather than details. A freestanding minimalist-type door unit (or window unit) that opens and closes may be built once and used for dozens of productions. Scenic templates, as well as color gels and gobos in lighting instruments, can create the appropriate mood. Merely changing pools of light communicates change in location. Changes in intensity and color may designate time of day. Channeling funds for major acquisitions in lighting and sound (which benefits the congregation at large) and costumes (used again and again) may present an initial financial burden, but not necessarily a long-term drain.

Remove Distractions

Rented backdrops that are professionally painted, rented decorations that are professionally constructed, or your own imaginative approach to eliminating distractions by minimally dressing an open stage replaces the theatrical mandate to build massive, conventional scenic structures. Whatever scenic offerings are made to the public on the stage must be free of distractions. *The stage space and surrounding areas of the stage must also be free of distractions.* Such distractions may include choir chairs or pews, chalkboards, an organ or piano, or anything that appears in the stage space but is not specifically called for in the playscript. An audience must be able to hear the spoken word and have unencumbered visual access to the actors on stage. This is why lighting, staging, costumes, and sound reinforcement (when applicable) may become your priorities. If church drama needs to set a pace for creative worship forms, then you should wisely strategize available funds and resources so that you build a nearly professional lighting, sound, props, and costume core with which to work.

STYLE AND CONSISTENCY

Style can be defined as that which governs the distinctions of a certain group or period. It relates to your directing of a play by translating your interpretative ideas to the audience. Your research of the play gave you insights into the world of the play. The world of the play is the play's **intrinsic style**, its environment, language, and action. The **extrinsic style** of the play is the interpretation of the play's action, your response to what the play means, its important moments, and the feelings solicited from the audience. Extrinsic style includes the scenic space of the stage, lighting, costumes, music, and the actors' movements, gestures, and voices. Your job is to mold all elements of the production into one consistent, unified idea. You will probably operate within two basic stylistic genres: historical realism and contemporary realism.

Historical Realism

Historical realism involves portraying the play in the period in which it was written. Biblical plays frequently deal with common Near-Eastern people of varying social classes. They frequently live ordinary lives and, through the action of the play, usually encounter a life-changing spiritual revelation. Historical realism of a Bible play helps an audience grasp the essence of life in a time past as it applies to the present. Historically accurate costumes of biblical plays reflect the geographical climate as well as the customs of a race and society, signifying a simple, nonmaterialistic life-style of the poorer classes. Head-coverings on female characters show their social position. The flowing wraps common to biblical costumes give a sense of the epic sweep that spiritual themes have had through the course of history.

Attempting to create a professional scenic setting for historical realism can be difficult, especially for a biblical play. As a rule of thumb for church drama directors, it is best not to try to replicate realism in backdrops or flats. Most backdrops that are painted by a nonprofessional are ultimately distracting and look nonprofessional. Poorly painted palm trees or pyramids or river valleys look like poorly painted palm trees, or pyramids, or river valleys. If this is the desired effect, great! But most of the time the desired effect is as much reality as possible. Unless you have a professional scenic painter and a considerable amount of money, dispense with portraying realism in a backdrop. Rent a professionally created backdrop, and make sure you have the correct rigging to mount it.

Instead of attempting to replicate realism, consider putting your energies and resources into set pieces, props, and costumes. Set pieces and props are things that surround the people and the human drama. They can be real whenever possible, not imitative or cheap looking. Spend time acquiring real props and set pieces. It takes very few real set pieces and props to communicate vividly the life of the drama and the world of the play. Do not fake it with poorly made do-it-yourself props. Poorly rendered props have the same effect as a poorly done backdrop. Rent, or borrow, or buy. Keep one staff member of the drama ministry organizing and administrating props ("running props"), especially during the last phase of rehearsals if not sooner.

Contemporary Realism

Contemporary realism is easier than historical realism because props, set pieces, and costumes consistent with the style are more accessible. But whatever the style of the play, keep making simple and consistent choices. This is probably the single best advice a beginning church drama director can be given concerning the style of a play: always make simple and consistent choices.

It would be good to have in your drama ministry a black back drape (or cyc) that can be mounted as a backdrop. Wing flats painted black, which are used to mask the offstage areas of the stage space, should also be a priority. If storage allows, you may need two on each side. As stated earlier, lighting and costumes, combined with set properties and hand props, will serve you best in making simple and consistent choices in style.

SET PROPERTIES

There are basically three functions of stage scenery: to provide a suitable background, to communicate important information, and to operate easily within the action of the play:

> Small objects handled by the actor on the stage are called hand props. They include such items as teacups, books, fans, letters, and many more similar items . . . Set properties are the larger elements more closely related to the scenery but still used by the actor. This group includes furniture, stoves, sinks, rugs, ground cloth, and any domestic object. Exterior set props consist of small rocks, stumps, bushes, foliage, dirt, grass mats, and so on. Set properties are in the care of the property person, who supervises the placing of the set prop on the stage and its removal to a stored position offstage.[1]

Remember to seek set properties that are realistic, not poorly made imitations. Stumps and rocks may be rented from a decorations house for a small fee. Use actual bookshelves, books, desks, etc., rather than painting a picture of them, unless the painted version is essential to the style of the production. There are only a few hundred professional scenic painters in the United States, and most churches do not have one among their congregation. Consequently, replace nonprofessional scenic painting with only essential set properties.

You may want to use set pieces called cutouts. Cutouts are commonly constructed of plywood and braced with 1 by 3s that frame and support the back. Cutouts may be likened to silhouettes in that they have irregular edges and may or may not represent something unidentifiable (clouds, cityscape, bushes, etc.).

Props List for *THE CARPENTER*

Preset on Stage

Living room—Act One

Upright piano— lid open	*Over it:*	Last Supper picture
Piano bench	*Inside:*	Sheet music
	On it:	Hymnal
Couch	*Over it:*	Norman Rockwell picture
	On it:	Rolled newspaper
		Afghan
End table	*On it:*	Lamp with fancy shade
		Dish of candy
		Bible
	Under it:	Box of magazines
Desk	*On it:*	Goose neck lamp
		Pencil holder with a pen and pencil
		Ink bottle
		Photo album
		6 books with bookends
	In middle drawer:	
		Writing tablet
		Letter opener
		Keychain with a number of keys
	In top left drawer:	
		3 business-size envelopes; addressed with stamps
Small desk chair		
Wastebasket to right of desk	*In it:*	Crumpled letter
		Banana peel

Bookcase	*On it:*	Framed photo of baby
		Vase with artificial red rose
	In it:	Almost every shelf (3)
		filled with books
		Bric-a-brac with books
	Over it:	Large framed scripture
		motto
Carpet		

Prop table—left entrance
  National Geographic
  Bible—worn black cover
  Vase of flowers
  White note-size envelope
  Rope

Prop table—center entrance
  Saw
  Dustcloth
  Candy box
  Feather duster

Twin Oaks Repertory Company
A Man for This Season
William Chelsea
Props Mistress: <u>Amy Spires</u>

Masking tape divides each prop storage area.
Use tape to label each area.

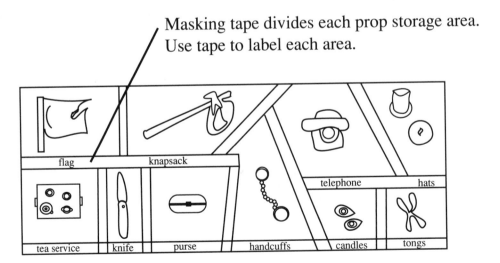

Example of a Prop Table

FLAT SCENERY

The basic element of a scenic inventory is the flat. Consisting of a muslin-covered wooden frame, the flat is painted to effect the scenery for one play, then painted again for the next. Constructing a flat is quite simple once you have decided its dimensions (4' x 8' for illustration):

Step One

Stiles are made of grade A white pine 1 by 3s cut to exactly 7 feet 9 inches. Rails are cut to 4 feet. Square the corners of the frame perfectly. Place the corner blocks (¼" plywood, 10" squares cut in half diagonally) ¼" from the outside edge of the rail and ¾" from the outside edge of the stile so that the grain runs across the joint. Attach with 1¼" clout nails. Fasten toggle bar in place with keystones (quarter inch plywood, 6 inches long by 3½" at the wider end and 2½" at the narrower end) and the corner brace with half keystones. Always allow ¾" margin from the outside stile edge to any corner block or keystone.

Step Two

Now turn the frame over and cover with unbleached muslin allowing 3" of extra muslin on all sides. Attach the muslin with tacks about 4 to 5 inches apart. Do not drive in the tacks all the way in the event of a mistake or desired change. Tack the inside edge of the stiles first, then tack the rails moving from the center out. Keep the muslin free of wrinkles but do not stretch it. Now drive in all tacks.

Step Three

Turn back the extra flaps of muslin. Apply a thick, even coat of adhesive (glue, whiting, and paste mixture) to the wood. Press the muslin firmly into place. After the glue has set, add a second row of tacks 8" to 10" apart and ½" from the outside of the flat. Trim off the excess muslin with a razor blade or carpet knife.

It is recommended that the first items you build for your scenic inventory should be two or four 4' x 7' or 4' x 8' flats and paint them black, to be used on each side of the stage to define the stage space, eliminate distractions, and mask wing areas.

The construction of a flat is a basic illustration of the construction of most stage scenery. Many of the other types of scenery, such as door flats, windows, cutouts, fireplaces, and hung scenery employ the same concepts and techniques but with a greater degree of specificity.

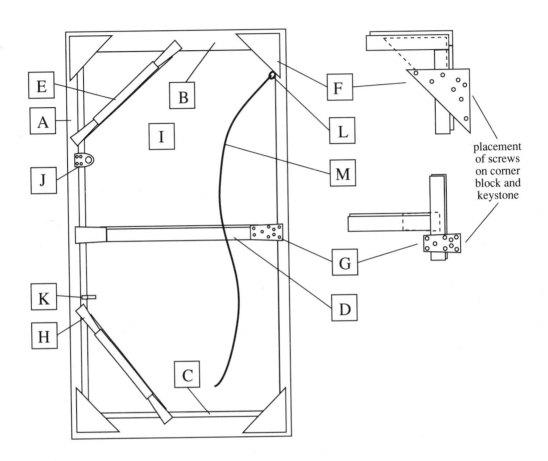

placement
of screws
on corner
block and
keystone

Example of Basic Flat

Basic framing techniques for the single unit of
framed scenery, the flat.

(A) Stile, (B) Top rail, (C) Bottom rail, (D) Toggle rail, (E) Brace, (F) Corner block,
(G) Keystone, (H) Split keystone block, (I) Canvas, (J) Brace cleat, (K) Lash cleat,
(L) Lash line eye, (M) Lash line.

Examples of Framed Scenery

(1) The framing of a set piece with profile edges, (2) Flat with profile edge,
(3) Window flat, (4) Two-fold flat with double-door opening, (5) Door flat.

Examples of Door Treatments

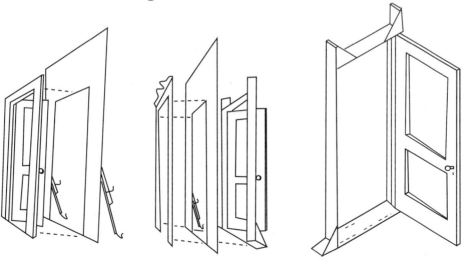

Platforms

Anyone can construct 6"-high risers and, by stacking them on top of one another, create a variety of levels. Some churches however, may have the resources for elevated levels for major action, stairways, or upstairs scenes. In this case, nonprofessional platforms are a standardized 4' x 8' platform unit, made of 2 by 4s and ¾" plywood, which can be combined with additional platforms as needed. Well-built platforms, however, are heavy, expensive, and cumbersome to store. Each church drama department is encouraged to communicate with all the necessary governing bodies of the church before venturing into a platform inventory. A few helpful illustrations that follow show some of the aspects of building platforms.

Examples of Parallel Platforms

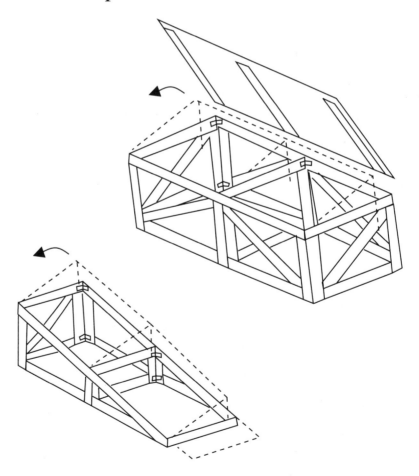

Example of an Irregular-shaped Platform

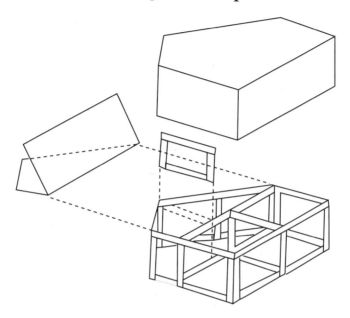

Examples of Stairs

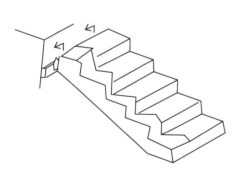

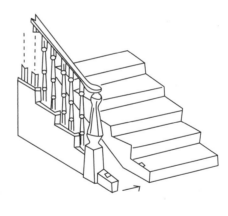

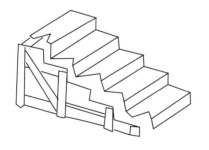

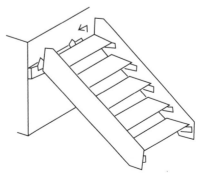

TWELVE

Lighting the Action

The need for visibility justifies the need for lighting in the church drama program. Other reasons for lighting the stage area include the ability to establish the mood of a scene, to communicate information such as the time of day, to emphasize areas on the stage, to create a set or scenic idea, and to punctuate the dramatic values inherent in the action or play.

Most Christian drama groups do not perform in a fully equipped proscenium stage. In fact, most groups present theatre in small auditoriums or recreation rooms, equivalent to thrust and arena staging configurations. Therefore, our basic purpose in theatrical stage lighting in Christian drama is illumination and the creation of atmosphere. Atmosphere is accomplished by the mixture of colors, keeping a fairly balanced intensity but varying levels of brightness. Illumination must be focused on the actors, not spilling over onto the eyes of the audience. This is achieved by mounting the instruments at a correct vertical angle or through the use of barn doors, a unit of four adjustable flaps placed on the front of the instrument to control undesired spill. The placement of a number of instruments both in front of, above, and from behind the playing area gives dimension (a sense of depth) to the actors.

There are three essential angles for lighting: vertical sources; outside positions (when an actor is on the outside of the stage looking outward); and inside positions (when an actor is upstage). In building lighting capability for the church drama ministry, begin by correctly lighting the participants in weekly worship services (e.g., the pastor and the choir). When this is accomplished, add lighting instruments that fill out the entire acting area for the largest production the auditorium will accommodate.

It is impossible to address here every lighting need of every reader. **Financial resources** determine lighting instrument acquisitions even when the congregation perceives the worth of professional stage lighting. Most importantly, a thorough knowledge of **electricity** is a prerequisite when considering a lighting plan.

Any approach to stage lighting belongs to a stage lighting professional. The first available money should be spent on a **consultation** fee with a lighting professional who will draft a master plan for your specific needs. If your drama program justifies the purchase of prograde lighting equipment, you must consider professional consultation. Consultation fees are the best way to spend the first dollars in the lighting area and are usually subtracted from the balance of the first purchase.

A professional can map out an intelligent long-range plan for your lighting acquisitions. He can educate your lighting technicians concerning dimmers, cables, rigging, wiring, color, direction, and focus.

This cursory treatment of lighting in this book does not do justice to the immensely complicated lighting elements of electricity, rigging and pipes, color, angles and aiming, dimmer boards, and computer lighting programs. Furthermore, the infinite needs and complex variables that each reader brings to this text cannot possibly be answered here. Seek a professional for all of your stage lighting business.

AIMS IN LIGHTING

In play production, two obvious but nonetheless important considerations should be constantly kept in mind—the audience must be able to hear and they must be able to see. The audibility of actors is greatly dependent upon their correct speech production, their projection, and the acoustics of the auditorium. Believe it or not, lighting is a factor in proper hearing too.

Lighting an acting area is not just a question of providing pretty colored lights for the audience to look at, nor is it only to illuminate the performers. It is much more than this. Lighting ought to intensify and emphasize the play's mood and dramatic impact.

Stage lighting is not an exact science. It is science in the service of performing art. Rules are very few, if indeed there are any. Provided that the lighting works with the other elements in the production to enable the playwright and the actors to communicate with their audience. Virtually anything goes. What can lighting do for a production? What are our aims when we employ light on the stage?

Illumination

Communication between actor and audience depends on sound and sight. The actor's complete body, especially eyes and mouth, are the means of communication, and all must be clearly visible if a character is to be projected. Everything in theatre interacts, and light is closely related to sound. The actor who is difficult to see will usually be difficult to hear.

So the first basic requirement of stage lighting is sufficient **illumination** to achieve positive visibility. But how bright is that? Light is a measurable quantity, but such photometric measurements have no place on the stage. One of the indications of theatrical doomsday will be the appearance of a lighting man with a photometer. Theatre is much too much of an interplay of mind and matter to be reduced to precise physical measurements. One must have confidence in the judgment of one's senses. If it looks right, then it is right.

Unless the auditorium is very, very small, perhaps up to about eight rows, the amount of light cannot be ideal for all seats. If there is enough light for the front row, it will be insufficient for the back. If the amount is correct for the back row, then it will be overbright at the front. This is assuming that all members of the audience have identical eyesight, which they certainly do not! The amount of required light also varies with the brightness that has gone before. The human eye contains a mechanism (the iris) to adjust eye sensitivity to varying light conditions. This iris mechanism is not immediate in response, and so the amount of light needed when the curtain goes up will vary with the brightness of the auditorium lights that have just gone out. The stronger the houselighting, then the stronger must be the opening stage lighting. An overture played with the houselights low or out and some lights to dress the curtain (or dress the stage if there is no curtain) gives all opportunity not only to prepare the audience's sound sensitivity but to adjust their light responses to the scale of the production's audiovisual palette.

Once the performance is under way, the required quantity of light remains related to what has gone before. A change from relative brightness to relative darkness must always take into account the time scale of change. A dark night scene that the audience has been watching for several minutes might be quite visible, but plunge them from a bright sunny scene into such a night, and they will require a positive measure of time to readjust—and in that time, communication may be lost and the magic theatrical spell broken. Within a static scene the amount of light is also relative. If one actor is brighter than another, it must be for a dramatic purpose. The seven-foot tenor in the chorus who always gets his head in the light becomes the unfortunate brightness reference point for the whole stage. The solution is usually not to increase the overall stage intensity to match the bright point, but to reduce this overbright part to balance with the rest of the stage. In a two-actor scene, it is often better to balance by reducing A rather than by increasing B. Balance is the key to the amount of light required. Brightness is relative rather than absolute. If the balance is good, lighting from a midpoint in the auditorium will ensure an acceptable level for both front and back rows. The wise lighting designer will use dress rehearsals to try all seats in the house.

Lighting quantity is only the very beginning of the stage lighting story. After (but only after) basic illumination has been provided, light can start to fulfill a more exciting role as a dramatic tool.

Dimension

In a conventional proscenium theatre where the audience sits in a block facing a picture frame stage, there is a tendency for the stage picture to appear rather flat with only two dominant dimensions: width and height. The third dimension, **depth**, is, of course, present but less obvious. This tendency toward apparent flatness increases as the size of the auditorium increases with a larger proportion of the audience seated further away from the stage. Indeed it is one of the reasons for enthusiasm for alternative theatre forms, where the stage thrusts into the audience or even, as in theatre-in-the-round, becomes surrounded by the audience.

The director, designer, and actor use many techniques to stress the third dimension and restore apparent depth to the production. Scenery can be built with an exaggerated perspective. It can be textured, and clever things can be done with the spacing of scenic pieces relative to one another. The director, often using several levels, groups his or her actors to emphasize stage depth. But the lighting designer can kill all this effort with one tiny wave of his magic wand. By pumping light flat on to the stage from the front—particularly from a low, near horizontal, angle—the stage picture can be given an appearance of total flatness.

With flat lighting, the actor's nose will not stick out, his or her eyes will not recede; the dancer's limbs will pirouette in a squashed oval rather than a true circle. But with correctly angled light, the actor can be presented as a natural three-dimensional human rather than as the pasteboard cutout figure that can be the inevitable product of proscenium staging. So we must strive for a dimensionally lit actor.

With flat lighting there is little point in designing dimensional scenery. Scenic wings, if receiving equal frontal light, will appear to run together; solid chunks will appear flat; and lumps of physical texturing will just not be visible. Solidity only becomes apparent when contrasts of light and shade are created by directional lighting. So we must strive for a dimensionally lit scene.

But a **sculpturally modeled actor** in a sculpturally modeled environment is not quite the end of the dimensional story. There can still be a tendency for such an actor to merge with the background. By use of light, partly from the sides but especially from the back, it is possible to enhance the illusion of depth in this relation of actor to background. It is a technique much used in the television studio because TV lighting, especially in black and white, has a major problem in restoring picture depth within the two-dimensional screen. The use of backlight streaming over the actor's shoulders may be difficult to justify on the smaller stage where there is usually already a shortage of equipment for the more basic requirements. Nevertheless, one chunky backlighting lamp can make all the difference to the appearance of the production's depth. So we must strive for a dimensional relationship between actor and scene.

Selectivity

In film and television the director can use his or her cameras to select the exact part of the action that he or she wishes the audience to concentrate upon at any given moment in the production. He or she can select any breadth of vision from a wide panorama to a closeup of a pore on an individual actor's skin. In theatre, the audience normally has the whole stage within their angle of vision at any one time; to focus attention to a particular area, the director can use light. The obvious technique is to light only the selected part of the stage while other parts are blacked out. However, it is also possible to make a subtle but positive selection of vision by balancing the selected area to a brighter level than the rest of the stage. It is surprising how effectively even a small light rebalance will help to **concentrate the audience's attention** on the appropriate action area.

Atmosphere

Perhaps the most fascinating and rewarding use of light is the possibility of influencing the mental state of the audience. The word *atmosphere* can cover a wide range of situations. It can mean something as basic as using light to tell the audience whether the action is taking place on an October afternoon or a July morning. But it can also mean something more subtle than mere weather forecasting. Light can help to control whether the audience feels happy or sad, extroverted or withdrawn, aggressive or submissive.

One of the principal ways of controlling such atmosphere is by mixing warm and cool light. Warm, gold, happy, cheerful at one end of the scale; cool, steel, and miserable at the other, but with a whole range of intermediate tones making a continuous range of emotional possibilities. Other ways include the balancing of light and shade. Exaggerated contrasts can induce a feeling of apprehension, even terror.

Light, of course, can only help to create atmosphere. Light never works by itself and is only one of a package of integrated staging devices that the actor and director use to control the emotional state of the audience.

Interaction

These stage lighting aims, illumination, dimension, selectivity, and atmosphere, are not unrelated. In fact they interact with one another to the point of positive conflict.

Atmosphere is often achieved by a partial lack of illumination. Selection of a tightly controlled area is most readily done by using a single spotlight. Dimensional lighting requires a series of angles from several spotlights whose beams, ending up on the floor, will increase the size of the selected area. Lighting for dimension can also lead to some loss of visibility unless the balance is very delicately controlled. And so on.

The adjusting of light in terms of one aim usually affects the others, and so the lighting designer has a little think loop whizzing round in his head during the time that he plans and executes his lighting design.

Can I see? Do I see a dimensional actor in a dimensional environment? Do I see the correct part of the stage action? Do I sense the appropriate atmosphere? Can I still see? Is it still dimensional? And so on.

At first one does this consciously, almost asking oneself verbal questions. But after a little experience the loop starts to accelerate, and very soon it whizzes round at something approaching computer speeds with a continuous assessment of all the interacting variables.

Fluidity

Stage lighting is not static. Throughout the time span of a performance, the selectivity and atmosphere of the light is fluid with changes of two basic types: conscious and subconscious.

Typical conscious selective light changes are an actor switching on a light or a rapid cross-fade from one side of the stage to the other. Atypical conscious atmosphere change is a quick fade to blue for a sentimental song. The audience knows that such changes have happened and indeed may even verbalize on the lines of "Ah, the lights are changing, the sun must be setting."

Subconscious changes are ones that the audience is not aware of, but that nevertheless influence their involvement in the production. An example of a subconscious selectivity change is the subtle shift in balance as the intensity is crept up a couple of points on one particular area and down a little on the rest of the stage. The audience's attention will be concentrated on the brighter area without realizing that anything has happened. Similarly, although the audience may not be aware of a slow, gentle increase of cool tone and decrease of warm, such an atmospheric shift will contribute subconsciously to the emotional effect that the actor and director are seeking.

Cynics have been known to mutter about the stupidity of having a hundred invisible cues. But these very cues are part of the greatest excitement of true theatre: the integration of acting and related staging devices to communicate at a subconscious level.

Pause for a moment to consider our role as audience. It is the one moment in our lives when we sit down, lay bare our souls, and authorize someone to tamper with our subconscious and to program our thinking. We even pay for the privilege! In our offices, factories, and shops, our daily work patterns and emotional responses could be controlled by similar methods including light. If this were done, we would, would we not, complain! To put it mildly!

Returning to theatre, the difficulty of light changes is that individual audience members differ in their sensitivity: not just in their response to the physical optics of light but in their general sensitivity, artistic, aesthetic, emotional, call it what you will. Thus a subconscious light movement must be very finely judged. It can never be just right for an entire audience: to some it will register consciously and to others it will penetrate not at all. This fine balance is a problem not merely for lighting. It is probably the basic problem of theatrical communication.

Style

There is a danger that these lighting aims could become a rigid definition of stage lighting. But theatre is not a rigid medium. There are almost as many different possible production styles as there are productions.

In a **naturalistic** production where the design aims at accurately detailed realism, the aim is to make all the lighting seem logical in terms of sun, moon, and table lamps. If it is a romantic play, there is much juggling with sunset, moonrise, and the switching of delicately shaded lamps in an attempt to create a selective atmosphere that is logical in terms of these light sources. If the play is farce with a complex plot, high illumination for total visibility is likely to be the prime consideration with the only difference between midnight and high noon being that the window curtains will be closed and the room ablaze with wall brackets, table lamps, standard lamps, or perhaps just one huge, but imaginary, center chandelier.

A play performed on a heap of black rostrums against a cyclorama will probably treat selectivity as top priority at the relative expense of other aims. If the production is conceived in terms of gauzes, smoke, and electronic music, then it is likely that the lighting style will emphasize atmosphere.

In an opera where there are lots of notes to the bar, the singers' faces will go through motions not unlike those of speech, and a reasonably naturalistic quality of illumination will help them to project. However, in one where there are lots of bars to the note, a more effective approach may be to use a very atmospheric light that does not illuminate the faces too clearly: the facial contortions required to produce sustained vocal tone are not always helpful in projecting character.

Similarly, in most dance situations, it is necessary to concentrate on dimensional lighting of the body as this is the dancer's principal means of dramatic expression.

Contemporary theatre has one school of thought—that the audience must be consciously involved in the drama. To such believers, anything savoring of subconscious romantic atmosphere is out. Lighting becomes a continuous all-revealing blaze of white. This like all other styles is just another possible way of approaching the conversion of a script into communicative staging—the tragedy for the theatre when any single style becomes clothed in dogma and its application to all situations becomes obligatory to the point of being a matter of doctrine.

Thus, different productions will use different mixes of the standard lighting aims, and the mix for any particular production will arise from the style of that production.

A Definition of Stage Lighting

Now we may be able to construct a possible definition of stage lighting. The words form a useful checklist of aims: Stage lighting is a fluid, selective, atmospheric, dimensional, illumination appropriate to the style of a particular production.

LIGHTING EQUIPMENT

Lighting equipment consists basically of the lights themselves and a control system. The number of lighting instruments and what the system can do will depend on financial resources available and whether you purchase or rent.

There are numerous types of instruments. The word *instrument* is used to describe an incandescent lamp housed in a metal casing that directs or focuses its beam. The instrument is connected by a cable to a dimmer board, which contains switches that can turn the instruments on or off and dimmers that can control the brightness of the light. Most instruments accommodate a color frame for holding color gels that affect the color of the light emitted.

There are three basic instruments that the average church drama group will want to consider: PAR floodlights, the ellipsoidal spotlight, and the Fresnel (freh-NEL) spot.

Ellipsoidal spotlight is a unit that provides a sharp beam of light that can be shaped by moving an aperture in the lens. The ellipsoidal (or Leko) is generally mounted in the audience area, above and in front of the stage. It has an excellent beam of 30 feet or more, making it ideal for use on light trees or mounted on a grid.

Fresnels are utilitarian floods giving a softer light. The beam is adjusted by barn doors (a shutter device that is attached to the instrument). Fresnels are best mounted above the stage or in front of the playing area. Their light throw is not more than 25 or 30 feet.

PAR lights (parabolic aluminized reflectors) are the most basic of floodlights. They are available in various beam spreads, from very narrow to very wide. PAR cans (the lamp looks like it is housed in a big coffee can) cannot be focused, but the axis of the beam spread can be adjusted by turning the lamp in the housing. PARs are comparatively inexpensive, good for a wash of light, but do not offer much flexibility.

A **scoop light** has no lens and is best used over the stage area or hung in the wings. It has a wide flood of light and is good for lighting a sky drop, a cyc, or the scenery.

Follow spotlights are large instruments mounted on a stand, designed for long throws of light—75 to 125 feet or more. Their primary function is to single out a performer such as in a musical. They provide special applications for a dramatic production.

Border lights and striplights all have their specialized purpose, frequently used to light backdrops and other areas when a great deal of unfocused lighting is needed.

Dimmer boards may be utilized when you begin using about six instruments, although every play has different requirements. Dimmers provide central control for activating each of the lights on an exact cue. Because it is not dramatically satisfactory for a stage light to snap on or off, a rheostat or dimmer is used to raise and lower light intensity. All of these necessities can be compactly arranged in a box called a dimmer board. The board and its operators may work backstage or in the rear of the house.

When renting or buying lighting equipment, many dealers will need to know:

1. The size of the acting area or stage. If it varies from production to production, they will need to have some indication of maximum and minimums.
2. The size of the auditorium and the audience seating configurations.
3. If 220 current is available and where?

4. How the instruments will be mounted?
5. Will the equipment be permanently installed?
6. Will the equipment need to be portable enough to take on a tour?
7. Anticipation of future growth and expansion.

Use of color is important since it adds light and mood. Stark white light is often too harsh, so gels are placed in frames and attached to the front of the spot lens to provide the desired effect. Obtain a ring of samples of Roscolux gels from your local light dealer. The most commonly used gel colors are "no-color blue," "bastard amber," and "no-color pink."

FIRST STEPS IN LIGHTING DESIGN

Let us look at the simplest possible situation. Starting with just one spot, one cable, and no dimmers, let us see how we can build up all-effective use of, say, the first 10 instruments.

We are moving away from objective scientific facts into an area of personal preference where no two individuals are likely to agree wholeheartedly. Theatre, like all art forms, is a matter for individual, personal, subjective response. There is no absolute objective standard for good lighting just as there is no absolute objective standard for good acting. So, as this is a personal opinion, I shall write as one thinking aloud.

I hope that nobody has to start as low down the scale as step one, but if anyone does, there is only one light to acquire and one place to put it. The spot is a **Fresnel**, and the position is **center** auditorium ceiling. The distance of the spot from the stage will depend on the width of the acting area and the beam angle of the spotlight. If we know any two of these we can work out the third. The simplest method is to draw the situation at a suitable scale such as one-quarter inch to the foot (50:1 if you are metricated). Knowing the spread and throw, the required beam angle can be read off with a protractor.

Spotlights are less effective when pushed to their limits of maximum and minimum beam angle. Spots can be spotted down from their maximum but not flooded bigger than it. So choose a slightly wider spread than your calculations suggest. Or, if you already have the spotlight, place it a little further from the stage than seems theoretically correct.

However, the limiting factor in placing a spotlight in the auditorium is rarely the lack of ability to choose the theoretically correct position. It is the difficulty of finding any position that is architecturally possible while being even remotely suitable. In the small hall, the problem is usually one of achieving sufficient height. If the light hits the actors at a near horizontal angle it will have, to put it mildly, a flattening effect. When the actor faces the audience, his or her eyes will have no depth and his or her nose will not stick out, a problem that increases with the distance between actor and audience and therefore not so vital in a tiny hall.

A bigger problem with horizontal lighting in any size of auditorium is that the shadows will be life-size. As the angle of light increases, the shadows will decrease until the point where the light is coming vertically from above the actor and the shadow is all contained within the area of the actor's feet and is therefore barely noticeable. But such a vertical light, if the only source, plays havoc with the actor's face. His or her eyes become black sockets and the highlighted nose assumes Cyrano de Bergerac proportions. Few actors use the nose as a principal means of dramatic expression, and their main acting features, eyes and mouth, are in darkness. The compromise angle to produce a visible sculptured actor, with a shadow of proportions that he can dominate, is somewhere within the range of 30 to 60 degrees.

Therefore the light is positioned with a view to fulfill two of the basic requirements of stage lighting: to make the action visible and to make it as dimensional as possible. Priorities are right by putting visibility first and foremost. There is no point in acting if the audience cannot see the actor. With only one source we are hardly in a position to use light to control the atmosphere. If the play is generally cheerful I would probably put in a bit of pale rose, and if it were sad I should go for the palest steel tint.

Light is an important way of selecting the area of the audience's vision and concentrating their attention upon the dramatically significant area of the stage. With but one spot, selection is limited to differentiation between stage and auditorium. This may seem obvious, but I have personally seen small theatres with quite large lighting rigs where this was not achieved and the light spilled all over the proscenium arch, the audience, and even the auditorium walls.

Our single spot must therefore be focused carefully so that the light is contained within the stage picture. If at all possible, the spot should have a barn door attached to shape the beam. If we focus to

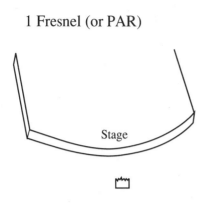

1 Fresnel (or PAR)

Stage

give sufficient width, we shall almost certainly have too much height; and the height of the light should be no higher than to catch the head of an actor standing at the back of the acting area.

If I have dwelt on the use of this single spot, it is because the principles outlined for this solitary source are the basic principles for getting the maximum out of any size of rig. When lighting I suppose that, as I focus each and every spot, I do a quick mental check on whether I am getting the maximum effect of *visibility, dimension, selectivity,* and *atmosphere.* Unless the rig is big (and certainly bigger than the situations discussed in this chapter), then this is probably also the order of priority.

If I had two spots only, I would place them both in the auditorium ceiling but would use positions toward the side of the auditorium rather than in the center. If the width between the side walls was not a great deal wider than the proscenium opening, I would put the lamps on the side walls, but if the auditorium was very wide, I would try to choose ceiling positions just a little farther apart than the proscenium width.

2 Fresnels (or PARs)

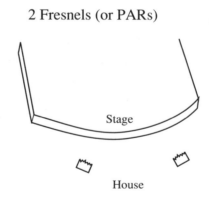

Stage

House

All our light is still coming from the front. The scene will therefore be rather flat. But because an actor is receiving light from both sides, he is at least a little bit more sculpted than when we had one spot only. We can increase this dimensional effect by putting slightly different tints in the spots, say gold in one spot and pale gold in the other—or perhaps rose in one and gold in the other, or, if it is a cool situation, perhaps steel in one and steel tint in the other. Other possibilities are gold and open white (i.e., no color) or steel and open white. It is all a matter of experiment. Playing with a couple of spots and a bundle of gels is the best way to find out about controlling the color of the stage picture.

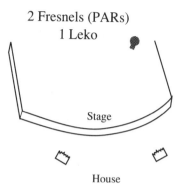

2 Fresnels (PARs)
1 Leko
Stage
House

With spot No. 3 it is time to go backstage, and perhaps it is time to introduce a key into the lighting: motivation. That motivation need not be a logical source such as moon, sun, or standard lamp, because it all depends on the style of the show that we are doing. It could be a spot shining through a window or it could be just a spot giving cross-light or backlight.

Back to the checklist! This lamp is really going to start doing something for dimension, and by changing colors during the show (think of access when you position the lamp) we can start getting *atmosphere* under control. If we are building up a rig by buying equipment, it is now time to acquire our first profile spot, which will give us more accurate control of the beam, and we can always get interesting effects by using gobos.

Another way of dealing with three spots is to have only one in the auditorium and to use the other two focused across the stage from positions immediately behind the proscenium. On the whole I prefer the two out front, but stage lighting is somewhat trial and error. It is only when you have such a small amount of equipment that you may have to experiment.

If I had four spots only, in the interests of balance, I would probably place two FOH (front of house) spots in the auditorium and the other pair immediately behind the proscenium to light across the stage. Keep them highish, because apart from considerations of keeping the actor dimensional and his shadow short, if the spots are too low one actor will tend to cut off the light from another actor.

By the time we are using four lamps, I would favor having all the FOH spots as profiles. This has rightly become standard practice because it en-

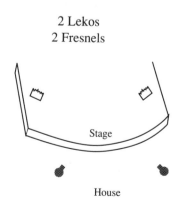

2 Lekos
2 Fresnels
Stage
House

ables us to contain the light within the proscenium arch and to trim the edges quite accurately by means of the built-in shutters. Moreover, profile spots have less spill outside the main beam and, after all, it is the actors that we wish to light, not the audience. Certainly I have suggested earlier that the first two spots should be Fresnels, but in a desperate situation (and you cannot get more desperate than lighting a play with one or two spots!) the Fresnel has width to its beam and is much easier to adjust.

With these four spots we have just the beginnings of selectivity, not the selection of clear-cut areas, but we could focus the audience attention to one side of the stage or the other—if we had dimmers. When do we start introducing dimmers into the scheme of things? If it is a question of buying, not yet. Renting? Yes. But I think spending money on dimming is relatively unwise until you have about six spots. Unless you are producing 19th-century romantic opera.

Buy spot No. 5 instead and use it for a key light.

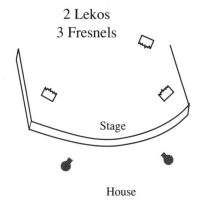

No. 6 could go center, immediately behind the proscenium. With two crossing spots, you are almost certain to have a dark hole in the middle, so the new spot can focus straight upstage. Perhaps not dead center for fixing or focusing: that will depend on the shape of the set. If you have some dimmers, you are now getting increased control of the area of stage that you would like the audience to look at. And as for visibility, the number of dark holes should be decreasing.

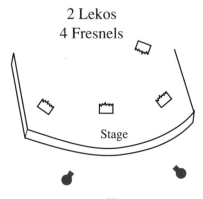

Spot 7 is a real breakthrough. Four spots behind the proscenium and we can really start talking about No. 1 spot bar without blushing! If we label the spots A, B, C, and D, an actor standing on the OP (actor's right) side of the stage would be lit by spots A and C, while an actor standing on PS (actor's left) would be lit by B and D. These spots will not do much for an actor standing immediately underneath them, but that position will be lit from the FOH. When we have only a few spots, the duty of the spot bar is to provide visibility upstage.

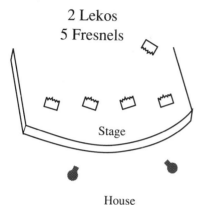

And yes, you are quite right, the onstage lighting is now getting out of balance with the FOH, so spot No. 8 should go out into the auditorium. Place it center where it can fill in the gap between the two lights on the FOH bar, which for architectural reasons have probably had to be positioned too far to the sides.

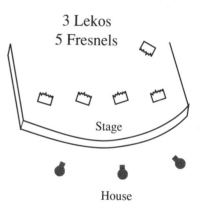

And spot No. 9 could be FOH also, so that we can carry on with our aim of lighting the actor from both sides to give him or her as much solidarity as possible. If we label these four FOH as W, X, Y, and Z, the actor who was lit by A and C upstage will be lit by W and Y when he or she comes downstage. If this were a programmed learning machine, the next question would be, What lights the actor stepping downstage from B and D?

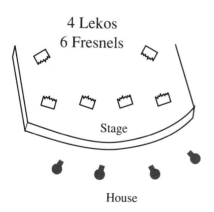

But this is not a defined factual recipe for lighting. It is just one man's thoughts, and anyone who has reached spot No. 10 by practical experiment will be so full of ideas that he will have dozens of possible uses for it. I think it is quite likely that it will find use as another key light, perhaps one from each side of the stage, or perhaps two keys from the same side with a difference of color or directional quality.

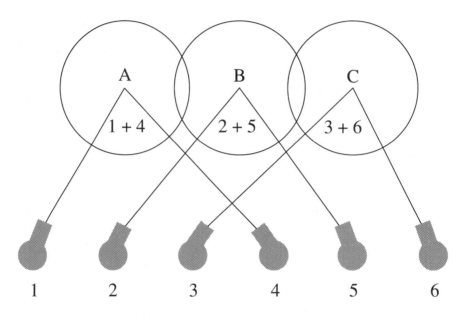

Common Aiming Technique: Fan Setting

With our 10 spots, we have quite an adaptable lighting rig. If you need to vary the stage atmosphere in terms of warm and cool tones, we could split our lamps into pinks and blues, or we could have mainly pinks with just a few blues, or perhaps some neutrals. There are lots of possibilities and much of the detail will be a personal response. But not too personal, the light must be relevant to the production style.

LIGHTING CUE SHEET

In some plays, once the lights are set there are no variations. General lighting is used throughout. At other times, it is necessary to highlight acting areas by reducing the intensity of other areas. This should be handled unobtrusively and with a light hand. The dimmer board makes these light changes possible.

A lighting cue sheet may be prepared as a separate form from the stage manager's promptbook. The sheet needs to include warning cues (when to start anticipating a lighting change) and the place in the script where the actual light change occurs.

Example of Lighting Cue Sheet

Park Springs Festival Productions
Play: DAVID
by: D. H. Lawrence
Operator: Linda Rasin

Act: I
Scene: i

CUE No.	LINE or ACTION	TIME	EXECUTION	NOTES
Preset	30 minutes before curtain		House 10 Stage 4	
1	Stage Manager "Go"	10 ct.	House ↓ 0 Stage ↓ 0	Stage behind house
2	Sound of Merab's tambourine	3 ct.	Full Stage ↑ 10	Preset Samuel's special No. 4
3	Jonathan ". . . And coming in anger"	slow 10 ct.	Full Stage ↓ 8	Extremely slow count
4	Saul ". . . Blessed be thou of the Lord!"	6 ct.	Special ↑ 5	Preset back borders No. 7
	etc.			

THIRTEEN

Costuming the Actors

Costumes may reveal more about the play and the characters than many other considerations, save the text. A costume conveys important information about social status, age, historical period, and geography. Audiences enjoy looking at costumes. They are undoubtedly one the richest sources for creativity in the dramatic production.

While it is difficult to cover in a few pages all the aspects of costuming, here are some general guidelines that may prove helpful in selecting fabrics for your costume inventory:

- Avoid using extreme color contrasts except for special dramatic effects.
- Use bright colors for accents and not on a person who is on stage most of the time.
- Combinations of primaries and their complementaries should be used sparingly.
- Use neutrals and pale colors on large people.
- Keep neutrals, grays, and browns away from the actor's face.
- Light colors and whites do not support the weight of dark colors above them.
- A small amount of bright colors will balance a quantity of neutrals. Combine them creatively.
- Use a single color and its shades for one costume.
- Enliven a dull scene with the use of color combinations.
- Consider the climactic build of the play by the addition of color.[1]

There are three basic categories of costumes: (1) special, which communicates a mood or idea; (2) modern, or contemporary realistic clothing; and (3) period, designs of garments from historical periods. Each category may be constructed with different fabrics, colors, and patterns. You must be careful that a costume is not anachronistic. Stiff silks and silk substitutes, such as taffeta or rayon taffeta, are not historically appropriate biblical costumes. Silk was only for the extraordinarily wealthy. Cheesecloth may be a useful for costume pieces such as veils or throws but usually must be dyed. Dyeing produces beautiful hues if you are equipped to dye fabrics. Other considerations include:

- Velvet and corduroy should only be used for intensely dramatic figures of royalty or a medieval church figure. Otherwise, do not use them in a biblical play.

- Use woolens, cottons, and cotton synthetics of all qualities and textures.

- Since many of the people of the Bible lived under the domination of foreign cultures (Egypt, Assyria, Babylon, Persia, Greece, Rome), and since much of Hebrew visual art and literature was destroyed, rely on three sources for costume information: (1) Assyrian and Egyptian sculptures; (2) specific references in the Bible; (3) and dress habits of modern Palestinian peasants.[2]

Note: If you are performing on a hollow wooden stage, which makes actors sound like they are stomping, have all soles of footwear and shoes rubberized (any shoe repair shop will do it). There are few things more annoying than not being able to hear dialogue because actors are pounding the floor with every step they take.

BIBLICAL COSTUMES

The most important thing to consider in choosing fabric for biblical costumes is the quality of its drape. When you drape the fabric, the folds that form should create curves, not straight lines. To understand this, drape a piece of knit fabric between your hands and compare it to draped taffeta.

Choose loose woven fabrics, lightweight cottons, and cotton T-shirt knits. Avoid stiff fabrics and polyesters. Prewash fabric to take out sizing.

Color choice is the next most important quality. Today's dyes are much sharper and more intense than in biblical times. Look for earth tones: all shades of browns, rust, beige, moss green, yellow ocher. While it is true that some garments were striped, don't overdo it. Muted colors will give a good overall effect, and deeper values or cooler colors will allow major characters to contrast and stand out.

The traditional biblical character should have the following costume pieces: tunic or robe (variations in cut and sleeves); overgarment (coat, aba, cape or pallium); headdress for men and women; and a sash or girdle (with a few beltless designs for variety and according to body shape).

Some actors may need armor. Armor is becoming expensive to build, buy, or rent. For the least expensive armor, write or call for a catalog from Tobins Lake Studios, Inc., 2650 Seven Mile Rd., South Lyon, MI 48178 (313-229-6666). For armor used by professionals, contact Costume Armor, Inc., P.O. Box 85, 2 Mill St., Cornwall, NY 12518 (914-534-9120).

For years now there has been a growing need for assistance in the designing and costuming of biblical plays and pageants. More and more churches are enlarging the scope of their Easter and Christmas worship services, and means are being sought to increase the dramatic effects. One of the easiest ways to acquire patterns for biblical costumes, angel wings, original costume designs, and specialty props is to purchase a pattern package from Irene Corey Design Associates. This package includes full-scale patterns with complete instructions, which when mixed and combined in different ways, will serve to costume an entire cast of biblical characters, including wise men, Pharisees, shepherds, soldiers, and angels. This may be the best money spent as you begin to assemble your inventory of costumes. For a complete catalog and information on the biblical pattern packages call or write:

Irene Corey Design Associates
5410 Worth St.
Dallas, TX 75214
214-821-9633
FAX 214-823-7574

Here are a few examples of costumes, arranged in chronological order. These illustrations will guide you toward choosing the correct patterns for the historical setting of the play.

BIBLICAL COSTUMES

Female

Female
(beltless)

Tunic, long; full sleeves
Veil over fitted scarf

Tunic, full; long sleeves
(unbelted)
Veil over fitted scarf

BIBLICAL COSTUMES

Male
(Jesus)

Male
(Priest)

Tunic, full sleeved

Coat, loose; full sleeved
(for Pharisee, prayer shawl
and veil)

ANGEL WINGS
(no harness)

Arm Wings

These wings are worn without a wing harness. The arms of the "angel" slide into a sleeve pocket, allowing for movement or variations of wing positions. This style is useful when the "angel" must enter into a restricted area, such as the baptistery.

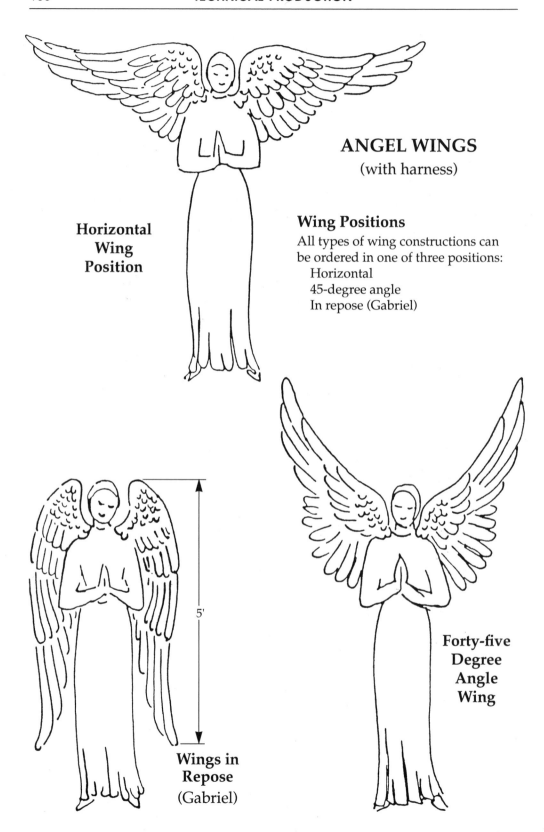

ANGEL WINGS
(with harness)

**Horizontal
Wing
Position**

Wing Positions
All types of wing constructions can
be ordered in one of three positions:
Horizontal
45-degree angle
In repose (Gabriel)

5'

**Wings in
Repose**
(Gabriel)

**Forty-five
Degree
Angle
Wing**

EGYPTIAN

Male

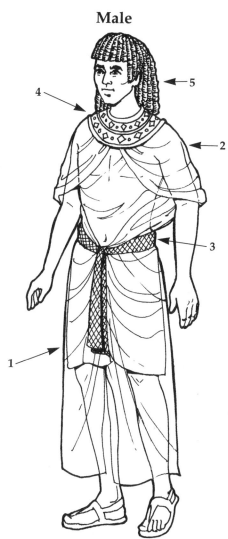

Female

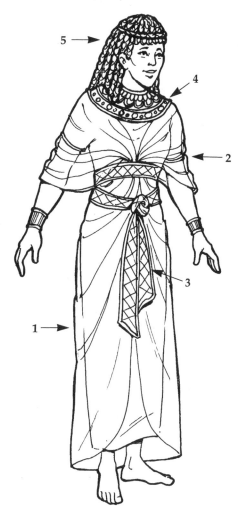

1. Wrap a linen loin skirt (called a *schenti*) and tie it or belt it just below the waistline.

2. Wear a sheer linen robe over loin skirt. You may want to wrap or tie it in place. (Called a *kalasiris*.)

3. Use a decorative sash or girdle to secure the skirt and robe.

4. Use patterned bands of metal and stone to make a wide decorative collar.

5. Wealthy Egyptians wore delicately styled wigs.

1. Construct a semitight fitting, sleeved (or unsleeved) gown.

2. Overlay sheath gown with a sheer linen tunic. Use creative ways to drape the kalasiris.

3. Use a sash to girdle the folds of the draped kalasiris.

4. See collar of Egyptian male. Vary the intricate patterns for a female.

5. Female wigs may have numerous braids.

GREEK

Male or Female   **Female**

1. Build a chiton to fasten over the shoulders.
2. Create a rectangular woolen mantle measuring 12 to 18' x 4 to 6'. Drape this himation in a variety of ways leaving the right arm free. This is called a himation.

1. Build a chiton to fasten with pins (fibula) at the shoulder. Pull the chiton over the belt to create a pocket of material (kolpos).
2. Include an overfold on the top of the chiton. This is called an apotygma.
3. Create a smaller himation to be draped as creatively as you can imagine.

ROMAN

Female

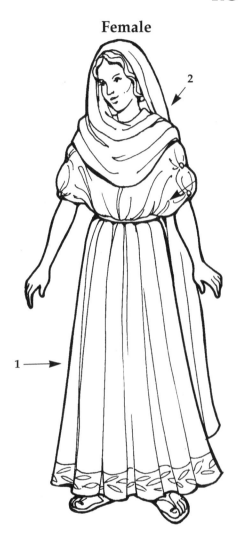

Male

1. After cutting a pattern of material for a chiton, build a seam from underneath the right arm to the hem. Pin the material along the top of the arm. (stola)

2. Wrap a rectangular piece of material for headcoverings and shawls. (palla)

1. Cut a simple rectangular pattern of material to make a tunic. Vary lengths as needed.

2. Fasten toga on one shoulder then allow it to hang and drape in a variety of ways.

3. Leather sandals should look authentic (not 20th century).

ASIA MINOR

Male

Female

1. Build a pair of braies to create semi-tight fitting leggings.
2. Cut a sleeved tunic. Vary the lengths from knee to ankle.
3. Construct a half-moon shaped cape called a paludamentum.
4. Use a decorative brooch to secure the paludamentum.
5. Place a decorative border on the inside of the paludamentum. Include decorative patterns to give authenticity.

1. Build a large belted tunic with generous sleeves. This is called a stola.
2. Construct a palla, a rectangular shawl draped or wrapped around the body in a variety of ways.
3. Research decorative patterns to embroider or applique for authenticity.
4. The headcovering should include a padded roll and a veil.

MEDIEVAL

Male

Female

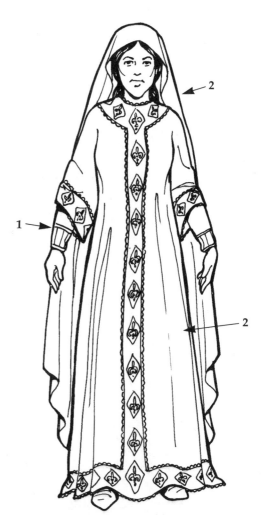

1. This tunic should have a full-cut skirt and sleeves.

2. Use braies similar to the ones used by an Asia Minor male.

3. Build a cloak that fastens on the right shoulder.

4. Add leather strips over the braies to add authenticity.

1. Construct a tunic as the primary full-length undergarment.

2. Drape a loose-fitting outer tunic with short sleeves and no belt.

3. Drape a rectangular piece of fabric over head.

REFORMATION

Male   ### Female

Beginning with costumes from Asia Minor, detail and authenticity may be beyond the ability of your costume crew. 16th-century costumes as shown here require even greater levels of expertise. You may want to consult catalogs of costume houses to become familiar with what is available for rental. Perhaps a nearby community college or university would allow you to rent some items from their inventory. Rent the "real" theatrical costume when you can.

REFORMATION

Male   **Female**

NUN   MONK   PRIEST

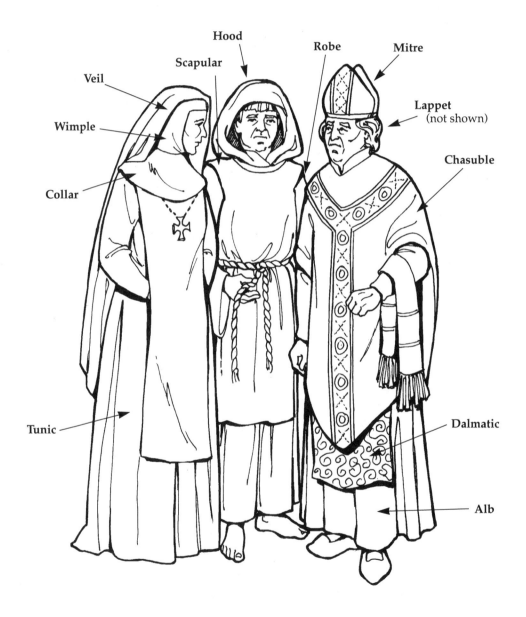

1600s

Female   **Male**

1700s

Male   Female

1800s

Female   **Male**

Character:

Name:
Work Phone:
Home Phone:

Ht.	Wt.	Shoe size	Age	Hair color

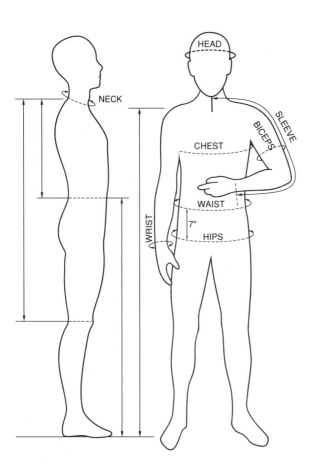

Head

Neck

Chest

Waist

Hips

Wrist

Biceps

Sleeve (center back of neck, around shoulder and elbow to wrist)

Neck to waist

Neck to knee

Waist to knee

Waist to floor

Shoulder to floor

Fill in measurements on figure.
Trace foot on back.

▶▶▶ FOURTEEN ◀◀◀

Makeup

Since we have been following a general persuasion to make simple and consistent choices, economy with realism, the area of makeup for the actor is also subject to the concept of "less is more." Except for age or character makeup, whenever an actor plays a character near his or her own age, little more than street makeup is needed. By this we mean that a woman may put on her normal types of highlights, color, and shadowing but in a little greater quantity for a more pronounced affect.

Your goal in technical production is to eliminate distractions and to make simple, consistent choices. There are few things more distracting than an actor who has applied an excessive amount of makeup so that his or her painted face looks grotesque even from the back row of the auditorium.

For an invaluable book on makeup, consult *The Face Is a Canvas: The Design and Technique of Theatrical Makeup* by Irene Corey (New Orleans: Anchorage Press, 1990).

DOING STRAIGHT MAKEUP

Ideally, all actors should learn to apply their own makeup. They can then project their personal ideas of the character's facial appearance, obtaining help from a makeup crew only on elaborate or difficult jobs.

The following material will introduce your actors to the basic principles of makeup. If you find this area fascinating and want to learn more, study an inclusive makeup text, or take a class in makeup.

Certainly you should **observe faces** of people around you, as well as scrutinize the untouched photographs of individuals in magazines such as *The National Geographic* and *Time.* Make mental notes of facial characteristics, contours, coloring. Observe portraits by such famous artists as Rembrandt, Vermeer, and Holbein for use of color, highlight, and shadow. To assist you in learning about faces, keep a "makeup morgue," or a file of picture clippings showing various people, different age-groups, etc.

Effective makeup requires good judgment and much experience. When you have learned the guiding principles, you must practice and experiment until you can skillfully and rapidly create plausible makeup of all kinds.

Whether you are working on yourself or other actors, the type of makeup you do for each role depends on five aspects: actor, character, play, theatre, and stage lighting. Since every actor's face is individual, you must modify makeup to fit the actor's particular bone structure, eyes, and coloring. If the actor looks almost like the part he or she is playing, apply "straight" makeup. If the actor must change his or her appearance to look like the part (older, fatter, thinner, younger), he or she needs "character" makeup.

The **role** itself provides clues to makeup. A character's age, health, occupation, personality, and attitude must be reflected in makeup. For example, a young character who plays tennis every day should have a ruddy or tanned face in order to look like an athlete.

The play's **style** also determines makeup. If the play is realistic, makeup should look natural to the audience. If the play is a fantasy, or if it is symbolic, etc., you may use limitless imaginative makeup to heighten certain features or to obtain special effects. Unusual colors, strange eyebrows, unique wrinkles and shadings may all be part of unrealistic makeup.

The **size of the theatre** has a great effect on makeup. If the distance between actor and audience is slight, as in arena theatre, makeup must be subtle. When the theatre is large and the audience is 100 feet or more away from the actors, makeup must be stronger and bolder if the actor's features are to carry. Of course, it is impossible for makeup to appear the same in all parts of the house. The makeup artist compromises by obtaining an acceptable effect in the first few rows, while yet assuring reasonable projection to the back rows.

The makeup artist should also consider the amount of stage light. Strong lights fade facial color. If you were to stand on stage under strong light and without any makeup, you would look completely "washed out." In order to project your natural coloring to an audience, males and females alike must have a tinted foundation, some rouge, and darker eyebrows.

Besides the amount of stage light, the source of light is important. Since we are used to the overhead light of the sun and to the shadows that it creates, any deviation appears strange to the audience. There-fore, when stage footlights are strong, or when side lights are used, makeup must replace the normal sun shadows.

Colored lights also affect makeup. Even though today's lighting technicians often use light pink and light lavender gels, there is usually more yellow in stage lights than in the sun's rays. To compensate, makeup adds the necessary red tints to the complexion, cheeks, and lips. Since stage lighting varies in each show, you must check all make-up under the actual lights and experiment until you obtain the desired effect. Remember, colored lights dim similar colors on stage and com-pletely darken complementary colors. For example, a red light subdues red makeup and makes green (red's complementary color) look black. Consequently, if you have red lights onstage, you'll need a heavy pink base and a rouge with a blue tint. If you have strong amber stage lights, apply rouge heavily and use a pink base, since amber "eats up" red. With blue lights the reds look purple or black, so for a blue moon-light scene use a light foundation and very little rouge. Since green light makes the face look ghastly, it is rarely used unless that effect is needed.

Now that you have seen how makeup varies according to actor, character, play, theatre, and lights, let us state the two general princi-ples of makeup application. One, always follow the basic lines, shad-ows, and highlights of the face you are making up, and then modify according to the character, play, theatre, and lights. Two, lighten areas that you want emphasized and darken those that you want subordi-nated. You will soon learn to apply these principles, but first you must equip yourself with the proper materials.

In the United States and Canada theatrical makeup is available from Stein, Max Factor, Mehron, Nye, Leichner, and Kelly. All have good products and many makeup artists patronize all. However, since each manufacturer numbers colors differently, it is usually easier to buy makeup from one company so that you become acquainted with their colors and identifying numbers. See what type your local drug-store carries, or order directly from a theatrical supply house or from the makeup companies. If possible, you should have your own indi-vidual makeup kit. Many actors outfit a metal fishing box or tool chest, or you may purchase a small student makeup kit from most of the makeup companies. If your church has its own group kit, your director may allow you to use it for practice. A word of caution. Makeup is expensive, so avoid being wasteful. Use only what is necessary and always screw on the caps tightly to prevent makeup from drying out.

Stocking a Makeup Kit

The following list contains the essential materials and basic colors that you will need in your makeup kit. For a list of all available colors, consult the catalogs of each makeup company.

- Foundation, often called base, gives the basic color to the face, neck, and ears, and when necessary to the arms, hands, and legs. Foundation colors suggest race, physical condition, age, and environment. There are three types of base: greasepaint (in tubes or sticks), pancake (a water base in cakes), and liquid (in bottles). Liquid foundation (sometimes called body makeup) is used for covering legs and arms.

- Liners or shading colors give the face a three-dimensional effect by providing shadows and highlights. The highlights or light colors advance and make areas seem larger; the dark colors or shadows recede and make areas appear smaller. Basic liners are brown, maroon, white, blue, and gray.

- Rouge helps to suggest age and physical condition. You will need moist rouge for applying directly on top of the base, and dry rouge for touching up after powdering. Choose medium red in both moist and dry rouge, as well as a moist reddish-brown for men's lips.

- Powder sets the makeup so that it won't smudge. Choose a shade lighter than the base, or use a neutral tone you can apply over any base.

- Eyebrow pencils darken eyebrows and provide eye lines. Use either medium or dark brown. Avoid black. It looks hard and artificial.

- Powder puff and powder brush. Apply powder with the puff and use the brush (a soft baby brush will work) to remove excess powder.

- Lining brushes. Use sable brushes to apply fine lines and wrinkles. Buy size $\frac{3}{16}$" for lines and $\frac{3}{8}$" or $\frac{1}{4}$" brushes for blending.

- Cold cream and facial tissue. Use for removing and wiping off makeup.

In addition to the above necessities, you may also consider having the following material available:

- Mold nose putty to make three-dimensional changes in the face, such as a different nose, a scar, etc.

- Wool crepe hair (for men) to make mustaches, beards, and sideburns. Crepe hair comes in yard length braids. Purchase gray-brown, light gray, and a color to match your own hair.
- Liquid latex to mold beards so that they can be reused. Spirit gum fastens the beard to the face. Rubbing alcohol or acetone removes spirit gum from the face.
- Spray colors for the hair and eyebrows. Apply with an old toothbrush.
- Large mirror, scissors (for cutting crepe hair), and mascara (to accent the girls' eyelashes).

Applying Makeup

The purpose of straight makeup is to make the actor more attractive or handsome by accenting his or her own features while overcoming any facial defects he or she may have, such as a face that is too long or a nose that is too short. The following is a guide for applying straight makeup on yourself, using a grease base:

1. **Clean your face** by removing all street makeup with soap and water. Contrary to what you may hear, do **not** coat your face with cold cream if you are using grease base. Modern grease base does not work well over cold cream.

2. **Apply the base**. For straight makeup you'll want a color that is a shade darker than your own skin. Dab forehead, nose, cheeks, chin, and jaw. Begin spreading the base over your face. Keep a light touch, applying the base on, not into, the skin. Blend from the center out in a smooth, even effect. Work up to the hairline, being careful not to coat the hair. Then cover your ears and entire neck with base. When you are through, rub a clean finger over your face. If the base comes off easily, or your finger leaves a print, you have used too much foundation and will have to wipe some off with a facial tissue. Your aim is a **thin** coating. A thick base looks bad and makes you perspire.

3. **Apply rouge.** Use sparingly—rouge goes a long way. Dot the rouge in a triangle shape at the highest point of each cheekbone. Blend with the fingertips toward the eyes, temples, nose, and jaw. The color should be strongest on the cheekbone and should grow weaker as it moves away until it blends unnoticed into the base. There should **not** be a sharp delineation. For a healthy glow, boys should carry rouge farther into the temples than girls, and farther down the jaw.

4. **Shadow and highlight the face.** This is called modeling. For straight makeup you will want to shadow the areas that are too prominent and highlight those areas that need emphasis. If your face is too wide, use a darker base on the sides. If your nose is too long, shadow the tip and highlight the ridge in a broad, short line. If your nose is too short, shadow the sides and use a narrow highlight on the ridge and over the tip. For a too-prominent jaw, dust under the chin with dry rouge, using a down powder puff or a rabbit's foot. Blend so that there is no definite demarcation.

5. **Accent the eyes** to make them look bigger and to compensate for the distance between actor and audience. If you surround the eyes with shadow, the whites of the eyes will look bigger by contrast, so darken the lids with brown shading that you **blend** and fade out gradually. If your eyes protrude too much, try shading with violet. If they are deeply sunk, highlight the upper lids with a lighter base. After you properly shade the lids, draw a fine eye line along the roots of the lashes with a dark brown pencil or with a brush and brown liner. Do not use black. On the upper lid start at the corner by the nose and follow close to the lashes, extending the line about ¼" beyond the outside corner. Powder immediately to prevent smearing. On the lower lids, start the line in the middle and draw it to meet the upper line at the outer corner. Eye lines are meant to look like heavy eyelashes. They should be attractive without drawing undue attention to themselves.

6. **Accent eyebrows** by darkening them if necessary. Using a medium or dark brown pencil, apply little feathery lines, drawn in the normal direction eyebrow hairs grow. The heaviest color should be near the center, with the brows tapering at the outer end in a line that parallels the curve of the eye. Keep a soft effect. You can lower eyebrows to make a nose look shorter. Block out the natural brows with base, or rub them with a cake of wet soap. When they are dry, apply base over them and then draw the brows a little lower. To make a nose look longer, raise the eyebrows slightly.

7. **Accent the lips.** Girls should use their own lipstick in a shade that matches the rouge. If their lips are an irregular shape (the lower or the upper lip too small or too full) cover them with foundation and then carefully paint and shape them with a lipstick brush. If one lip is larger than the other, use a darker shade of lipstick on it and a lighter shade on the smaller lip. If males need to accent their lips

they can either softly outline them with a brown pencil, or apply a brownish-red moist rouge that they then gently wipe off, leaving only a suggestion of color. Males should avoid accenting a cupid's bow of the upper lip.

8. **Apply powder** to set the makeup so it won't smudge. Be sure you are through with your makeup before you powder, as there is little you can correct once the powder is on. Pat on ample powder. **Do not rub.** Apply thoroughly and evenly. Then brush off excess powder with a soft baby brush. If necessary, touch up the cheeks with dry rouge. Girls may wish to apply mascara to darken their eyelashes. You may need to powder between scenes if you perspire and your makeup becomes shiny.

If you use a pancake base instead of a grease base, apply moist rouge, shadows, and highlights directly to your clean face. Apply heavily enough to show through the base. Then with a moist sponge, carefully stroke on a thin coating of pancake. Touch up your cheeks with dry rouge if necessary. Do not powder.

Always be careful of using too much makeup. You want your makeup to carry to the house without looking like Indian war paint. Too much is worse than too little! Apply only what you need. Many amateurs use far too much. Once your makeup is approved, leave it alone, despite what well-meaning friends or relatives say.

It is extremely "amateurish" to appear outside of the theatre while wearing stage makeup or your costume. As soon as the play is over and curtain calls are complete, remove your makeup with cold cream and facial tissue. Close your pores by splashing cold water on your face.

Some young actors believe that stage makeup will cause their face to break out. This is highly unlikely, unless they are allergic to all cosmetics. Excitement, tension, or worry about a part, however, may cause skin problems. If you clean your face before putting on makeup, and then remove the makeup immediately after performance, you should have no complexion problems from the makeup.

CHARACTER MAKEUP

Character makeup involves changing the actor's facial appearance to fit a particular role in the play. Since a person's face discloses his or her personality, emotional experiences, age, health, and attitude, it is

necessary to understand these aspects before you begin doing a particular makeup.

Intelligent observation of the faces you see in life will provide you
with numerous ideas for makeup. There are many ways to disclose
character. You can make the eyes, which are one of the most expressive
parts of the face, appear larger. You can make them appear farther
apart to suggest unfriendliness, or appear sunken for an ominous or
threatening attitude. You can change eyebrows to show character, by
raising or lowering them, or by making them look thinner or bushier.
The following sketches indicate a few of the eyebrows you can create.

You can vary nose proportions with shadow and highlight, or
with nose putty that creates a three-dimensional change such as a huge
or misshapen nose or one with a big bump on it. You can alter the size
of the mouth and change its expression by painting the corners up to
suggest happiness, or painting them down to indicate sadness, pain, or
meanness (notice the comedy and tragedy masks). You can add wrinkles to show the age or the emotional experiences of the character.
When using wrinkles always accent the natural lines on the actor's
face. Have him or her frown, smile, etc., and then while he or she holds
that position, outline his or her natural wrinkles with liner.

Most character makeup involves changing the face to look older.
From your observations you will note that as people grow old, specific
changes occur. The complexion becomes more sallow or pale, the facial
muscles sag, and the skin on the cheeks and neck becomes loose. Wrinkles appear, teeth may fall out, the lips usually become thinner, and the
hair gets sparse and gray. In addition to these changes, the face now
readily shows the type of life the person has led. If the person has constantly been cross or worried, there will be more pronounced frown
wrinkles in the forehead and above the nose than will a person who
has been generally happy. The happy person's wrinkles will fall at the
corner of the eyes and in the laugh lines that extend from the nose to
the corners of the mouth.

Of course, age occurs gradually and in your makeup you must
guard against making everyone look either young or ancient. Actors
playing people in their 40s and 50s need different makeup from those
playing people in their 60s or 70s or 80s.

To make an actor look in his or her 40s, use a more sallow base
than for youth and apply darker rouge lower down on the cheeks to
indicate the beginning of sagging facial muscles. Use less lipstick on
women and use brown liner for the men's lips. Model subtle pouches

under the eyes and wrinkle the outer eye corners. You may slightly gray the hair at the temples.

To make an actor appear in his or her 50s or 60s, lighten the base and use little if any lipstick. Eye pouches should be more pronounced. Indicate facial hollows and sags with brown shading and subtly highlight them with white. Emphasize wrinkles in the forehead, around the eyes, and from the nose to the mouth. Gray the hair at the temples, with a few gray streaks elsewhere.

Old age makeup requires a pale base and a face that is shadowed and highlighted to convey the sagging facial muscles and the loose cheek and eye skin. The wrinkles that appeared in the 50s are now deep and pronounced. The eyebrows are bushy and both they and the hair are white. Let us discuss the makeup for thin old age and fat old age. You can then modify these suggestions when doing middle-age makeup. Remember, the following hints should serve only as a guide. You must vary treatment according to individual faces and characters. For example, on a thin face adapt thin old age makeup.

For **thin old age,** apply makeup according to the following steps:

1. Apply a pale base.
2. Using maroon or brown liner, with brush or fingertips shade the:
   a. eye sockets (these should have the heaviest shadows).
   b. indention below cheek bones.
   c. temple hollows.
   d. side of nose.
   e. mouth corners.
   f. under jaw and chin.
   g. depressions on both sides of throat cartilage.
3. Using maroon or brown liner (do not use pencil) draw wrinkles where they naturally form in the:
   a. forehead.
   b. between the eyes.
   c. outer eye corners (called crow's feet lines).
   d. curved smile line from nose to mouth corners.
   e. vertical lines below and above the lips.
4. With white liner, highlight above all the wrinkles.
5. Using white liner, above each shadow, highlight the:
   a. bones over the eyebrows.

    b. cheekbones.

    c. chin point.

    d. line of lower jaw.

    e. throat cartilage.

6. With your fingertips carefully blend together the edges of high-light, shadow, and base. The effect should be subtle. Avoid the stark wrinkle lines that plague many amateur jobs.

7. Thin the lips by applying foundation over them. Allow only a small thin portion of the natural lip coloring to show.

8. Whiten hair and eyebrows. Make the latter bushy by brushing them the wrong way.

9. Powder the makeup.

10. Apply the beard and mustache, if needed.

11. Make up the hands by shading the depressions with gray or brown and highlighting the bones with yellow or white.

12. Properly arrange the character's hair.

For **fat old age:**

1. Apply a pale grease base that has a pink tinge.

2. Using maroon or brownish red liner, shade crescents:

    a. under the eye.

    b. under the cheekbones.

    c. between the cheekbones and nose.

    d. on lower cheek jowls.

    e. around the chin.

    f. at mouth corners.

    g. on throat

3. Add crow's feet and forehead wrinkles.

4. With white, highlight the wrinkles and shadows, including:

    a. the center of each cheek.

    b. each side of the forehead.

    c. under the eyebrows.

    d. on the eyelids.

    e. under each eye (for puffiness).

    f. on top of nose.

    g. on the chin bone.

h. the lower front of each cheek (to suggest jowls).

5. Blend edges of highlight, shadow, and base so there is no definite demarcation line.

6. Make the mouth appear larger by applying reddish brown rouge; highlight the lower lip with a lighter color in the middle.

7. Whiten hair and brows.

8. Powder face with a powder having a pink cast.

9. Apply beard and mustache, if needed.

10. Properly arrange the character's hair.

Beards and Mustaches

Many male characters must have beards or mustaches. Before you apply a beard, observe men who have them. You will notice that facial hair has certain boundaries, and that it grows forward under the chin and downward at the sides. It is thinner where the growth starts and becomes thicker farther down on the face.

To make beards, prepare the crepe hair the day before. Unbraid the amount and colors you'll need. To straighten the kinks, dampen the hair, put it between two towels, and press it with an iron. Since beards are rarely one solid color, combine the colors needed and then comb the pressed hair.

Below is a step-by-step procedure for applying beards:

1. Be sure the face is shaved and the part to be covered is free of greasepaint.

2. Define the bearded area by applying the adhesive. If you want to use the beard several times, apply liquid latex. Otherwise, use spirit gum. Put on two coats, allowing each to dry.

3. Hold a small piece of crepe hair in your hand and cut the ends on the bias. Do not use too thick a piece of hair, but have it longer than the desired finished length.

4. Paint the third and last coat of adhesive just above the larynx and apply a layer of hair, sticking it out toward the front. Hold until it is dry. Latex dries quickly. If you use spirit gum, press the layered hair firmly with a towel until the adhesive is dry.

5. In this same manner, cut the hair, apply the adhesive, and work up in layers—like shingles on a roof—until the front of the chin is covered with hair pointing down.

6. In this same manner, work up in layers on each side.

7. When completed, hold the beard firmly and gently comb out any loose hairs.

8. Trim to the desired shape.

9. At the top of each beard, you may need to pencil in hairs to blend the beard's edge so that it looks natural.

10. To remove latex beards, lift up one edge and gently pull off. Powder the back of the beard so it won't stick to itself. Trim off the rough edges of the latex. When you use the beard again, attach it with spirit gum. To remove spirit gum, use rubbing alcohol or acetone.

When making a mustache prepare the crepe hair and the face as for beards. Then:

1. With brown pencil draw the desired outline of the mustache.

2. Cover the area with liquid latex or spirit gum. Allow two or three coats.

3. Cut crepe hair on a bias.

4. Start applying the hair at the outer corner of the lip and work in several layers toward the center, following the lip line. With the scissors, hold each layer in place until dry.

5. Hold firmly and comb out loose hairs.

6. Trim. If you need to shape the ends, first apply a little spirit gum to the hair.

For an unshaven appearance, stipple gray-blue liner on the face with a sponge, or cut crepe hair about ⅛" long and apply evenly over the area with spirit gum.

Hair

The hair is an integral part of makeup, often providing by itself the character's credulity. Females can style their hair according to the overall image of the character. Color can usually be sprayed on. Hair can be slickly combed, messy, or bouffant, and it can be parted in various ways, etc. Males should avoid having a haircut close to performance, for it makes them look like "skinned rabbits" from the stage. Actually, males should have a haircut three to four weeks before performance and then they should let their hair grow till after the show. Since wigs are expensive to rent and difficult to fit, avoid their use if possible. For sketches on period hairstyles, see Appendix E in Richard Corson's *Stage Makeup*.

Putty

Nose putty can be used on any part of the face. Prepare the putty by molding it with greased fingers until it is soft and pliable. Then:

1. Clean the area to be covered.
2. Apply a coating of spirit gum.
3. Place the putty over the gum, forcing it down until it sticks.
4. Smooth out the edges until they blend into the face.
5. Cover the putty with base and any other makeup needed.
6. To remove, pull a thread tightly and run it along the area, under the putty.
7. Save the putty for reuse.

You can use nose putty to make scars, since most scars are welts. Build up the center of the scar in an irregular shape. Smooth down the edges. Color the raised surface with gray-blue liner. If indentations instead of welts are desired, apply three or four coats of collodion directly to the skin, drying between each coat. Collodion will give a drawn, indented look. Remove collodion with acetone.

Miscellaneous Considerations

To make teeth look like they are missing, use black tooth wax. Place the wax between the teeth unless several teeth are to be blackened. Then place the wax directly over the teeth.

In fantasies and in abstract or symbolic plays, stylized makeup is often used. Pictures and your own imagination will provide you with many makeup ideas. The following stylized types are presented only as suggestions:

Clowns usually have a white base and imaginative facial shadings with red, blue, green, etc. Their mouth and nose are often large. The eyebrows are unusual and there are imaginative markings around the eyes. The base may be pink. Their lips may be small and red with a definite cupid's bow. The eyebrows may be arched and often are painted black. Use green, blue, or violet eye shadow and two small dots of rouge on the cheeks.

Pirates need a dark base with eyes heavily shadowed for a sinister look. Emphasize their cheekbones, add a scar, and black out some teeth.

Elves often have turned-up noses and round open eyes. Use your imagination for eyebrows, markings, and ears.

Use the following page to reproduce for your actors as they create their makeup design.

MAKEUP PLOT

Eyes		Cheek	Nose	Mouth	Prosthesis

Base	Shadows	Highlights	
Eyeliners	Powder	Hair	
Note:			

Notes

Introduction

1. H. R. Rookmaaker, *Art Needs No Justification* (Downers Grove, Ill.: InterVarsity Press, 1978), 38-40.

2. Cheryl Forbes, *Imagination: Embracing a Theology of Wonder* (Portland, Oreg.: Multnomah Press, 1986), 168.

3. *The Oxford Companion to the Theatre*, 1983 ed., s.v. "Drama."

4. Northrup Frye, *The Great Code* (New York: Harcourt Brace Jovanovich, 1982).

Chapter Two

1. Victor Seymour, *Stage Director's Workshop: A Descriptive Study of the Actor's Studio Director's Unit* (Unpublished Ph.D. diss., University of Wisconsin, 1965), 57-75.

2. Lawrence Stern, *Stage Management: A Guidebook of Practical Techniques* (Boston: Allyn and Bacon, 1987), i-ii.

Chapter Three

1. Carl Allensworth, *The Complete Play Production Handbook* (New York: Harper and Row, 1982), 20-21.

2. Robert Cohen and John Harrop, *Creative Play Direction*, 2nd ed. (Englewood Cliffs, N.J.: Prentice Hall, 1982), 305.

Chapter Four

1. Analysis of Paul McCusker's *Family Outings* (Lillenas, 1988) courtesy of Deborah Craig-Claar. For additional concepts and practical suggestions in directing, consult Craig-Claar's work *What to Do with the Second Shepherd on the Left: Staging the Seasonal Musical* (Lillenas, 1992).

2. Great debt is owed to David Grote for his book, *Script Analysis* (Belmont: Wadsworth, 1985) in which he clearly shows directors how to analyze effectively each detail of the playscript, as outlined in this chapter.

Chapter Five

1. Cohen and Harrop, *Creative Play Direction*, 104-22.

2. Ibid., 139.

3. Alexander Dean and Lawrence Carra, *Fundamentals of Play Direction* (New York: Holt, Rinehart, and Winston, 1941), 111-53.

4. Cohen and Harrop, *Creative Play Direction*, 130-34.

5. Ibid., 135.

6. Dean and Carra, *Fundamentals of Play Direction*, 172-90.

7. Francis Hodge, *Play Directing: Analysis, Communication and Style*, 2nd ed. (Englewood Cliffs, N.J.: Prentice-Hall, 1982), 86.

8. Seymour, *Stage Director's Workshop*, 57-61.

9. Alfred Anthony Rossi, *A Critical Study of the Philosophy of Theatre and the Techniques of Stage Direction of Tyrone Guthrie* (Unpublished Ph.D. diss., University of Minnesota, 1965), 152.

Chapter Six

1. Dean and Carra, *Fundamentals of Play Direction*, 191-94.

2. Ibid., 200-202.

3. Ibid., 203-23.

4. Kathleen George, *Rhythm in Drama* (Pittsburgh: Pittsburgh University Press, 1980), 241.

5. Dean and Carra, *Fundamentals of Play Direction*, 231-42.

6. Ibid., 244-52.

Chapter Seven

1. This basic concept is attributed to Maria Ouspenskaya.

2. For advanced acting theories and techniques, read Michael Chekhov's *On the Technique of Acting* (New York: HarperCollins, 1991). For a complete anthology of acting exercises see *Acting Through Exercises* by John L. Gronbeck-Tedesco (Mountain View, Calif.: Mayfield Publishing, 1992).

Chapter Eight

1. Kristin Linklater, *Freeing the Natural Voice* (New York: Drama Book Publishers, 1976), 22-23.

2. Edith Skinner, *The Seven Points for Good Speech in Classic Plays* (Mill Valley, Calif.: Performance Skills, 1983), 7-26.

Chapter Nine

1. Harry E. Stiver, Jr., and Stanley Kahan, *Play and Scene Preparation: A Workbook for Actor and Directors* (Boston: Allyn and Bacon, 1984), 9-34 passim.

2. Grote, *Script Analysis*, 123-33.

Chapter Eleven

1. Owen Parker and Harvey K. Smith, *Scene Design and Stage Lighting*, 4th ed. (New York: Holt, Rinehart, and Winston, 1979), 325-26.

Chapter Thirteen

1. Allensworth, *Complete Play Production Handbook*, 290-91.

2. Lucy Barton, *Costuming the Biblical Play* (Boston: Walter H. Baker, 1937), 13-35 passim. Also consult Katherine Strand Holkeboer's *Patterns for Theatrical Costumes: Garments, Trims, and Accessories from Ancient Egypt to 1915* (New York: Prentice Hall, 1984).

Glossary of Stage Terms

ABOVE. To be farther upstage of someone or something.

ACT CURTAIN. The curtain that is opened and closed to mark the beginning and end of an act.

ACTION. The development of the story or plot.

AD LIB (*ad libitum*—at pleasure). Any lines or business improvised by an actor.

AESTHETIC VALUES. Those values in the production that appeal to the audience's sense of beauty or fitness.

APRON. The part of the stage that extends out beyond the proscenium arch.

AREAS (playing). Those parts of the stage, usually marked by a single piece or a group of furniture, that are suitable for the playing of a scene.

AREAS (stage). Those parts of the stage resulting from its arbitrary division into six areas (nine if the set is exceptionally deep).

ARENA. The type of theatre in which the audience sits on all sides of the stage.

ASBESTOS. The flameproof curtain immediately behind the proscenium that can be dropped instantly in case of fire to cut off the stage from the auditorium. (Not usually required in newer theatres having better exit facilities.)

ASIDE. A speech that is addressed directly to the audience on the assumption that the other characters on the stage cannot hear what is being said. Used frequently in plays of the 17th, 18th, and 19th centuries and in some modern plays to give the audience information the author found it difficult to convey in ordinary dialogue.

BABY SPOT. A small spotlight having a lamp of 250 to 500 watts and used to illuminate areas not more than 15 to 20 feet away.

BACKING. A flat or double flat used to mask the area behind a door, window, or other set opening.

BACKING STRIP. A strip of lights usually of low wattage, used to light the backing so that the offstage area will not appear to be a dark cave.

BACKSTAGE. The whole area behind the stage, including the dressing rooms and green room, used by the actors and other members of the company.

BARN DOOR. A four-shutter device that fits into the color-frame holder of a Fresnel spotlight to shape the beam and reduce scatter light.

BATTEN. Either a long pipe or a long strip of wood used to hang scenery, lights, or draperies. Normally it is supported by lines dropped from the gridiron and tied off at the pin rail. Battens are also attached to the top and bottom of drops. They are also used sometimes to stiffen two or more flats hinged together to form a wall.

BELOW. To be downstage of someone or something.

BIT or BIT PART. A small speaking part.

BLACKOUT. To take out all the lights on stage at the same time.

BOARDS. An old-fashioned term used to designate the stage. An actor was said to have "trod the boards."

BOOK. Ordinarily refers to the promptbook.

BOOM or BOOMERANG. A tall vertical pipe with a heavy base, usually of cast iron, to which spotlights or floodlights are attached. Frequently employed next to the tormentors.

BORDER (cloth). A narrow strip of canvas or muslin or velour hung above the stage and spaced so that the audience is prevented from seeing up into the flies.

BORDER (light). A strip of medium-wattage lamps in a metal trough and hung above the stage to provide general lighting to blend in the light from the various spots. Sometimes called the *X-ray border* when located just behind the teaser.

BOX SET. The standard interior set showing three walls of a room, with the fourth wall removed so the audience can see what is taking place.

C CLAMP. A clamp used to attach a lighting instrument to a pipe batten.

CALL-BOARD. A bulletin board near the stage entrance on which all information of importance to the cast or crew is posted.

CEILING PLATE. A special type of hardware used for hanging ceilings.

CLEAT. A *brace* cleat is attached to the stile of a flat so that a stage brace can be used to support the flat. *Lash* cleats are attached to the stile of a flat at several points to accommodate the lash lines that will fasten the flat to another flat.

CLOUT NAIL. A special type of soft iron nail that can easily be clinched. Used with corner blocks and keystones in the construction of flats.

COLOR FRAME. Used on spotlights and occasionally on floodlights to hold the color gelatins. Usually of metal.

CORNER BLOCK. A triangular piece of profile board or three-ply board used to join the stiles and rails of a flat.

COUNTERFOCUS. The director's use of one or more characters in a group to focus on someone other than the emphatic figure in the scene. Used to achieve variety.

COUNTERWEIGHT. A sandbag or cast-iron weight used to balance the weight of a piece of scenery hung from a set of lines. The counterweight makes it possible for a single fly man to raise or lower a heavy piece of scenery.

COVER. To come between another actor and the audience.

CROSS. To move from one place to another on the stage.

CUE. The word or piece of business at which point an actor is expected to begin speaking or begin some action. Also, the word or business at which point some crew member is expected to take an action.

CUE SHEET. The sheet of paper on which the stage manager or light man or sound man has written his cues.

CURTAIN CALL. The reappearance of the cast after the final curtain has fallen to acknowledge the audience's applause.

CURTAIN LINE. The final line delivered by an actor before the curtain falls. Sometimes called the *tag line*. Also, the imaginary line on the stage floor where the act curtain strikes it.

CUTOUT. A piece of scenery cut out of profile or beaver board to represent trees, bushes, buildings, hills, or other objects in silhouette.

CYCLORAMA (CYC). A large curved drop or curved plaster wall partly encircling the stage and lighted to simulate the sky. Also sometimes (wrongly) used to designate the set of velour or duvetyn drapes used to enclose the stage.

DEAD PACK. The stack of scenery that has been struck and will not be used again during the performance.

DIMMER. Any device for controlling the brightness of a lighting instrument.

DOCK. The place where flat scenery is stored.

DOUBLE TAKE. The delayed reaction of an actor when he or she finally realizes the significance of something he or she has heard or seen.

DOWNSTAGE. The front of the stage.

DRAMATIC VALUES. Those values in a play that are likely to evoke an emotional response from the audience.

DRAPES or DRAPERIES. A set of heavy cloth wings, borders, and back curtain that enclose the stage and prevent the audience from seeing the back or side walls. Used as a background for concerts, recitals, speeches, and occasionally for plays.

DRESS STAGE. A direction sometimes given to an actor to move slightly to balance the stage or to avoid being covered by another actor.

DROP. A large piece of canvas (or muslin) hung from a batten and painted to represent the sky, a landscape, a street scene, or the back wall of a room.

DROP SCENE. A short scene following a climactic scene that serves the dramatic function of lowering the tension that has been generated so that the next build can begin at a lower level.

DRY-BRUSH. To paint with a brush that is almost devoid of paint. Used to get the effect of wood grain, old brick, or rocks.

DUTCHMAN or STRIPPER. The narrow canvas strip (usually about 4 inches) used to cover the joint when two flats are hinged together. Also, the wooden strip (jigger) inserted at one joint when three flats are hinged together. The wooden Dutchman makes it possible to fold the three flats compactly so they can be moved easily.

EFFECT. A visual or aural illusion, intended to suggest rain, smoke, lightning, thunder, a doorbell, a train whistle.

EFFECTS MACHINE. Any device used to produce a visual or aural effect, such as a thunder sheet, a wind machine, or a crash box.

ELLIPSOIDAL SPOT. An efficient spotlight with an ellipsoidal reflector, especially useful in lighting the front areas of the stage from an overhead beam or the front of the balcony.

EXIT LINE. The last line spoken by an actor before leaving the stage.

EXPOSITION. Information regarding previous events that the audience must have in order to understand the action of the play.

EXTRA. A walk-on or a person added to increase the size of a crowd.

FEED. To deliver a line in such a way that the next actor can achieve the maximum response from his or her line, usually a comedy line.

FEEDER LINE. The line that is intended to set up the following line.

FLAT. A flat piece of scenery consisting of a wooden frame covered with canvas.

FLOODLIGHT. A lighting instrument throwing a wide beam of light that is directional but unfocused.

FLOOR CLOTH. The canvas or other heavy material used to cover the acting areas of the stage.

FLOOR POCKET. A recessed metal box in the stage floor that has several electrical outlets and is permanently connected by cable to the switchboard.

FLY. To suspend scenery or lighting instruments by lines from the gridiron.

FLY GALLERY. A raised platform along one side of the stage where the lines used to fly scenery are controlled. (Not ordinarily found in modern theatres.)

FLY LOFT or FLIES. The area above the stage where scenery is flown.

FLYMAN. The stage hand who handles the lines used to fly scenery or lights.

FOLLOW SPOT. A high-wattage, variable-focus spotlight usually located at the back of the balcony or in a projection booth and used to follow the movements of a singer or dancer on the stage.

FOOTLIGHTS (FOOTS). A metal trough housing a number of low-wattage lamps and located on the stage floor near the front of the apron. Its purpose is to blend and tone the light from the spots and remove the shadows from under the eyebrows and noses of the actors.

FORESTAGE. *See* Apron.

FOURTH WALL. The imaginary wall that has been removed from a realistic box set to permit the audience to view the activities in the room.

FRESNEL. A stepped lens that efficiently throws a soft-edged beam of light up to 25 or 30 feet. Commonly applied to any spotlight having this type of lens.

FRONT. The entire area of the theatre in front of the apron. Sometimes refers to the audience.

GAG. An exaggerated line or piece of business designed primarily to elicit laughter from the audience. A *running gag* is the repetition of the gag at intervals, usually with added refinements to increase the laughter.

GO UP. Expression referring to an actor who has forgotten his next line.

GATE. The optical center of an ellipsoidal spotlight where the shutters are located and where a masque, or gobo, can be inserted.

GAUZE or SCRIM. A drop made of theatrical bobbinet, cheesecloth, or other thin, loosely woven material and used in front of a set to give an air of unreality to the action taking place behind it. Also used behind a window or other set opening and lighted to achieve the effect of fog or distance.

GELATIN. A paper-thin sheet of colored plastic used in a color frame attached to a spot or flood for the purpose of coloring the light emanating from that source.

GIVE. To grant the emphasis to the most important actor in a scene.

GOBO. A metal cutout placed in the gate of an ellipsoidal spot to project a pattern or an image on a wall or drop.

GREEN ROOM. The room near the stage used by actors and crew members before or between acts to wait for cues or to go over lines or business.

GRID or GRIDIRON. The steel framework at the top of the stagehouse to which are attached the headblocks and pulleys that support the lines used to fly the scenery or lighting instruments.

GRIP. A stage hand.

GROUND PLAN. The plan of the set, including the placement of furniture, that has been worked out by the director and designer.

GROUND ROW. A long, low flat or series of flats used to mask the base of a sky drop and the horizon strips that light it or to suggest distant mountains, a nearby hedge, or a city skyline.

HAND PROPS. Those properties that actors handle or use such as glasses, food, letters, and the like.

HOLD. To wait for the laughter to fade before speaking the next line. Also, to wait briefly for a laugh to develop before delivering the next line.

HOLDING THE BOOK. The function of the prompter.

HOUSE. The entire area in front of the footlights. Also used to describe the audience.

HOUSE LIGHTS. The lights that illuminate the auditorium.

HOUSE MANAGER. The person in charge of all activities taking place in the house and related to the audience.

INNER, or FALSE, PROSCENIUM. The two tormentors and the teaser, which together serve to cut down the size of the proscenium opening to the dimensions required by the scene designer. Usually located right behind the act curtain.

JACK. A triangular brace that is hinged to a flat or set piece and is opened out to provide support or closed for storage.

JIGGER. *See* Dutchman.

JOG. A slight offset in a wall created by a narrow (1- to 2-foot) flat set at right angles to the other flats.

KEYSTONE. The small piece of profile board used to join a toggle bar to the stile of a flat.

LASH CLEAT. The steel cleat attached to the stile of a flat to accommodate the lash line.

LASH LINE. The piece of sash cord or clothesline used to lash one flat to another— usually at a corner of the set.

LEG DROP. A drop that is cut out in the center so that it can serve as a cloth or foliage border in the center of the stage as well as wings at either side.

LEKO. A term commonly used to designate an ellipsoidal spot.

LEVEL. Any platform or other raised portion of the stage.

LIGHT BRIDGE. A narrow platform suspended by lines just behind the teaser on which can be mounted spotlights, border lights, or other equipment. A pipe batten is used for this purpose in most modern theatres.

LIGHT PLOT or LAYOUT. A scale drawing including the ground plan of the set with the type and location of each lighting instrument and the area it is intended to illuminate.

LINES. The dialogue of the play. Also, the sets of lines used to hang scenery and lights.

LINNEBACH PROJECTOR. A wide-angle projector used to project an image on a drop from the front or rear.

LIVE PACK. The stack of scenery still to be used in a performance.

LOFT. *See* Fly loft.

MASCARA. If black, a substance applied to eyelashes to darken them; if white, applied to hair or eyebrows to whiten them.

MASK. (verb) To conceal a person or a piece of business from the view of the audience. (noun) The covering worn on the face by actors in Greek plays and occasionally in modern plays.

MUGGING. Grimacing; or, playing too obviously to the audience.

OFFSTAGE. All areas of the stage that are not included in the set.

OLIO. A painted drop of a street scene or garden that used to be hung well downstage so that a scene could be played in front of it while the scenery was being changed behind it. Rarely used in the contemporary theatre.

OLIVETTE. An old-fashioned, cumbersome, and inefficient type of floodlight.

OPEN UP. To turn toward the audience.

OVERLAP. To begin speaking before another actor has finished.

PACE. The rate at which a scene or act is being played. (*See* Tempo.)

PACING. Usually refers to an actor walking nervously about the stage —generally in a set pattern.

PARALLEL. A platform support that is constructed so that it folds up for easy storage or transportation.

PARALLEL SCENE. An expository scene in which there is no conflict. The characters proceed along parallel paths.

PERMANENT SET. A set that is divided into several smaller sets to represent the various locales of the play.

PIN CONNECTOR. The standard two-prong fiber connector used to join cables and lighting instruments.

PINRAIL. The heavy, firmly anchored rail or beam at one side of the stage to which the lines from the gridiron are tied.

PIPE BATTEN. The metal pipe that is usually attached to a set of lines hanging down from the grid and to which the scenery to be flown is fastened by snatch lines.

PLACES. The command given to the actors by the stage manager when he is ready to start the performance or begin an act.

PLANT. To implant in the mind of the audience an awareness of an event that may occur or an object that may be used at some later time in the play.

PLOT. The arrangement of the episodes of a story so that they produce the strongest emotional impact on the audience. Also used to designate the arrangement of lighting equipment or properties, as in *light plot* or *prop plot*.

PLOT LINE. A line of dialogue that is important to the audience's understanding of the action.

PLUG. (verb) To overemphasize a line or piece of business. (noun) The small flat inserted in a door flat to convert it to a window flat or a fireplace flat.

POINT. To provide additional emphasis to a line or piece of business.

PRACTICAL. An adjective applied to any property or piece of scenery that is expected to work or be used by the actors.

PROFILE. The British term for an ellipsoidal spot.

PROJECT. To make the voice carry to the entire audience.

PROJECTOR. An instrument for projecting a static or moving image onto a screen, a drop, or a wall.

PROMPT. To give an actor his or her line (or a key word) when he or she appears to have forgotten it.

PROMPTBOOK. The book kept by the stage manager (or director) in which all business, cues, and pauses are noted. It is usually held by the prompter during the performance.

PROPS or PROPERTIES. Every article on stage except the scenery. Furniture, rugs, draperies, or pictures are known as *set* props. Letters or food are known as *hand* props. Those hand props used by only one actor such as a pipe, watch, or eyeglasses are sometimes called *personal* props.

PROSCENIUM. The arch that frames the stage opening.

PUPPETS or MARIONETTES. Small doll-like figures that are animated by strings or by the hands.

RAIL. Either the bottom or top crosspiece of a flat.

RAKE. To alter the axis of the set so that it is no longer parallel to the curtain line. Also, to angle the upstage ends of the side walls inward to improve the sight lines of the upstage areas.

RAMP. A sloping passageway leading from a lower to a higher level; used in place of steps.

REPERTOIRE. The plays that are ready for performance by a repertory theatre.

REPERTORY. A term used to describe a theatre company that has two or more plays ready for production at any given time and plays them on alternate dates on a regular schedule.

RETURN. A flat that is set upstage of the tormentor and parallel to it, and used to narrow the stage opening still more. Normally it is attached to the downstage end of the side wall of the set and extends offstage far enough to mask the backstage area from view.

REVOLVING STAGE. A large circular stage that is set into the permanent stage floor or on top of it and can be turned by hand or by machinery. It has the advantage of permitting another stage set to be assembled in back while the first set is being shown to the audience. Then by revolving the stage, the second set becomes visible.

RHYTHM. The regular recurrence of accented beats and the arrangement of unaccented beats in the lines or movement or action of the play.

ROUTINE. The arrangement of musical numbers or scenes in a revue or musical comedy.

RUN. To move scenery (usually flats) by sliding it across the stage floor rather than carrying it.

S HOOK or KEEPER. A hook in the shape of a flattened S used to hold a stiffening batten in place behind two or more adjoining flats.

SANDBAG. A canvas bag filled with sand and used to counterweight the scenery being hung from the grid or to weight the empty lines so that they can be lowered to the stage when scenery is to be attached.

SCENE DOCK. The place where flat scenery is stored.

SET or SETTING. (noun) The arrangement of scenery to provide a background or environment in which the action of the play can develop. (verb) To repeat the lines or business of a scene until all of the actors have it firmly set in their minds.

SET PIECE. A single piece of scenery used alone or in conjunction with another set piece to suggest the environment in which the action of the play is supposed to take place.

SET PROPS. Those properties that are visually a part of the set such as furniture, draperies, pictures, and the like.

SHIFT. To strike the scenery for one set and set up the scenery for another.

SHUTTERS or BARN DOORS. Movable metal flaps attached to the front of a spotlight that can be adjusted to shape the beam of light emanating from the instrument.

SIDES. A set of typed and bound pages (usually half the size of a typewriter page) containing all of the speeches and cues of one character in a play.

SIGHT LINES. Those lines of sight from the sides of the auditorium and from the rear of the balcony that determine how much of the stage can be used so as to be visible to all parts of the audience.

SILL IRON. The strip of iron that runs across the bottom of the opening in a door flat and keeps the flat from spreading.

SIZE or SIZE WATER. Glue water used for mixing with dry pigment to prepare scene paint. Also applied alone to new canvas to provide a suitable base for painting.

SNAP LINE. A strong cotton cord impregnated with colored chalk and snapped against flat scenery to mark a regular design of wallpaper or paneling, which can then be filled in by a painter.

SNATCH BASKET. Any kind of hand basket used by a prop man to gather up small props from the stage during a shift.

SNATCH LINE. A short line used to attach a piece of scenery to a pipe batten for the purpose of flying it.

SOFTEN. To play down or de-emphasize a line or piece of business that is too obvious.

SOLILOQUY. A speech, usually longer than an aside, in which the audience is allowed to overhear what a character is thinking.

SPATTER. To apply paint to scenery in small dots by slapping the brush against one hand.

SPIKE. To mark in chalk or tape the position of furniture or scenery on the stage floor.

SPOT or SPOTLIGHT. An instrument that throws a focused beam of light on a relatively small area.

STAGE BRACE. An extendible wooden brace with metal fittings used to brace flats or door casings from behind to keep them from shaking.

STAGE LEFT. The left side of the stage as determined by an actor standing in the center and facing the audience.

STAGE MANAGER. The person who is responsible for running the entire performance from opening curtain to final curtain call.

STAGE POCKET. *See* Floor pocket.

STAGE RIGHT. The right side of the stage as determined by an actor standing in the center and facing the audience.

STAGE SCREW. A large screw turned by hand that is used to fasten a stage brace or a foot iron to the stage floor.

STAGE WAIT. An interval during which nothing dramatically significant is happening on stage. Should be avoided.

STEAL. To draw the attention of the audience from the actor to whom the scene rightfully belongs. Also, to move unnoticeably upstage or downstage or to one side in order to dress the stage.

STIFFENER. A stiffening batten used to stiffen two or more flats that have been joined together.

STILES. The vertical members of a flat.

STRAIGHT PART. A part in which the actor is playing very close to his or her own age and type.

STRIKE. To take down and remove a set from the stage.

STRIPLIGHT. Any type of lighting instrument in which several lamps are set in a metal trough. Usually applied to low-wattage lamps used to light backings or illumination at the base of a cyclorama or sky drop *(horizon strips)*.

STRIPPER. *See* Dutchman.

SUPER or SUPERNUMERARY. An extra or walk-on having no lines.

SWITCHBOARD. The lighting control board containing the switches and dimmers that control all the lighting instruments used in a production.

TAG or TAG LINE. The final line or phrase of an act or, more especially, of the play.

TEASER. The long horizontal flat hung directly behind the act curtain, which in combination with the vertical tormentors constitutes the adjustable inner proscenium.

TELESCOPE. To overlap the speeches of several actors so that they are all delivered at the same time.

TEMPO. The speed at which a given scene or act is played, especially the speed at which the accented beat recurs.

THICKNESS PIECE. The piece of wood (or other material) applied to an arch or doorway to give some indication of the thickness of the wall through which the opening has been made.

THROW AWAY. To deliver a line so that, though still audible, it is given the least possible emphasis.

THRUST STAGE. A stage that extends out into the auditorium so that the audience sits on three sides of the actors.

TIMING. Delivery of a line or execution of a piece of business to gain the maximum dramatic effect.

TOGGLE BAR. Any supporting crosspiece of a flat other than the top and bottom rails.

TOPPING. A method of achieving build in a climactic scene by having each actor deliver his or her speech at an increase in pitch and intensity over that of the preceding actor.

TORMENTORS. The two vertical flats just behind the act curtain that can be moved either onto or off the stage to adjust the width of the stage opening. In combination with the teaser, the tormentors form the inner, or false, proscenium.

TRAP. A trapdoor in the stage floor through which actors can enter or exit.

TRAVELER. A draw curtain that opens from the center and is suspended from a track.

TRIM. (noun) The draperies, curtains, pictures, and bric-a-brac included in a set for aesthetic rather than practical reasons. (verb) To adjust a drop or border so that it hangs straight or at the correct height.

UNCOVER. To move from in front of another actor so that he is visible to the audience.

UNIT SET. A set with certain permanent features such as arches or columns that, by the addition of doors or draperies or windows, can be made to serve as the background for all the scenes in a play.

UPSTAGE. Toward the rear of the stage. Also, to move upstage of another actor so that he must turn away from the audience in order to address you.

WAGON STAGE. A stage on wheels or casters that permits a set to be prepared offstage, then pushed onto the stage to replace another set on another wagon stage. Facilitates a much faster change of scenery.

WING IT. To proceed with a performance even though the actor is unsure of his lines. Presumably he will get whatever assistance he needs from the prompter in the wings.

WINGS. Flats or drapes located at the side of the stage and set parallel to the footlights to mask the offstage area; used mostly in outdoor or musical sets. Also, those areas offstage to the side that are masked by the wings. As a general term, used to designate all areas at the sides of the stage.

WORK LIGHT. A single unshaded lamp either on a stand or suspended from the flies to provide illumination for people working on the stage.

X-RAY BORDER. The name sometimes given to the first light border behind the teaser. Also called the first border or the *teaser* border.

Selected Bibliography for Directors

Works that may serve as a basic, core library are in **bold** print.

Directing

One of the best sources for information or availability of theatre arts books and scripts is **Drama Bookshop, 723 Seventh Ave., 2nd Floor, New York, NY 10014; (212) 944-0595.**

A Director Prepares. Stanley L. Glenn. Encino: Dickenson, 1973.

A Sense of Direction. William Ball. New York: Drama Books, 1984.

Acting and Directing. Russell J. Grandstaff. Lincolnwood: National Textbook, 1990.

Basic Drama Projects. Fran Everett Tanner. Caldwell: Clark Publishing, 1987.

Creative Play Direction. Robert Cohen and John Harrop. Englewood Cliffs, N.J.: Prentice-Hall, 1974.

Directing a Play. Michael McCaffery. New York: Schirmer Books, 1988.

Directing Drama. John Miles-Brown. London: Peter Owen, 1980.

Directing in the Theatre. High Morrison. London: Pitman, 1973.

Director's Theatre. David Bradby and David Williams. New York: St. Martin's, 1986.

Directors on Directing: A Sourcebook of the Modern Theatre. Toby Cole and Helen Krich Chinoy. New York: Bobbs-Merrill, 1953.

First Reading to First Night. Malcolm Black. Seattle: University of Washington, 1975.

Fundamentals of Play Directing. Alexander Dean and Lawrence Carra. New York: Holt, Rinehart, and Winston, 1941.

Golden Ages of the Theatre. Kenneth MacGowan and William Melnitz. Englewood Cliffs, N.J.: Prentice-Hall, 1959.

Improvisation for the Theatre. Viola Spolin. Evanston: Northwestern University Press, 1963.

Michael Chekhov's To the Director and Playwright. Charles Leonard. New York: Harper and Row, 1963.

On Directing. Harold Clurman. New York: MacMillan, 1972.

Oral Interpretation. Charlotte Lee and Timothy Gura. Boston: Houghton Mifflin, 1987.

Play Directing: Analysis, Communication, and Style. Francis Hodge. Englewood Cliffs, N.J.: Prentice-Hall, 1971.

Play Direction. John Dietrich and Ralph Duckwall. Englewood Cliffs, N.J.: Prentice-Hall, 1953.

Play Production and Direction. Charles Lowell Lees. New York: Prentice-Hall, 1948.

Play Production. Herning Nelms. New York: Barnes and Noble, 1950.

Prospero's Staff. Charles Marowitz. Bloomington: Indiana University Press, 1986.

Rehearsal. Miriam Franklin and James Dixon. Englewood Cliffs, N.J.: Prentice-Hall, 1983.

Script Analysis. David Grote. Belmont: Wadsworth, 1984.

Sense of Direction. John Fernald. London: Secker and Warburg, 1968.

Stage Direction in Transition. Hardie Albright. Encino: Dickenson, 1972.

Staging Premodern Drama: A Guide to Production Problems. Lee Mitchell. Westport: Greenwood Press, 1983.

The Art of Directing. John Kirk and Ralph Bellas. Belmont: Wadsworth, 1985.

The Art of Play Production. John Dolman, Jr. New York: Harper, 1928.

The Complete Play Production Handbook. Carl Allensworth. New York: Harper and Row, 1973.

The Craft of Play Directing. Curtis Canfield. New York: Holt, Rinehart, and Winston, 1963.

The Director as Artist. R. H. O'Neill. New York: Holt, Rinehart, and Winston, 1987.

The Director at Work. Robert Benedetti. Englewood Cliffs, N.J.: Prentice-Hall, 1985.

The Director in a Changing Theatre. J. Robert Wells. Palo Alto: Mayfield, 1976.

The Empty Space. Peter Brook. New York: Atheneum, 1968.

The Essential Theatre. Oscar Brockett. New York: Holt, Rinehart, and Winston, 1984.

***The Small Theatre Handbook.* Joann Green. Harvard: Harvard Common Press, 1981.**

The Theatrical Image. James Clay and Daniel Krempel. New York: McGraw-Hill, 1967.

***Theatre Games for Rehearsal: A Director's Handbook.* Viola Spolin. Evanston: Northwestern University Press, 1985.**

Acting and Actor Training

A Voice for the Theatre. Harry Hill. New York: Holt, Rinehart and Winston, 1985.

Acting and Stage Movement. Edwin White and Marguerite Battye. New York: Merriwether, 1985.

Acting in Person and in Style. Jerry Crawford and Joan Snyder. Dubuque: William Brown, 1983.

***Acting Is Believing.* Charles McGaw. New York: Holt, Rinehart, and Winston, 1966.**

***Acting Through Exercises.* John L. Gronbeck-Tedesco. Mountain View, Calif.: Mayfield Publishing, 1992.**

Acting with Both Sides of Your Brain. Ramon Delgado. New York: Holt, Rinehart and Winston, 1986.

Acting with Style. John Harrop and Sabin Epstein. Englewood Cliffs, N.J.: Prentice-Hall, 1982.

Acting: An Introduction. Derek Bowskill. Englewood Cliffs, N.J.: Prentice-Hall, 1977.

Acting: Handbook of the Stanislavsky Method. Toby Cole. New York: Lear, 1947.

***Acting: The First Six Lessons.* Richard Boleslavsky. New York: Theatre Arts Books, 1933.**

Active Acting. Leslie Abbott. Belmont: Star, 1987.

Actors on Acting. Toby Cole and Helen Krich Chinoy. New York: Crown, 1949.

***An Actor Prepares.* Stanislavsky. New York: Theatre Arts, 1936.**

Audition. Joan Finchley. Englewood Cliffs, N.J.: Prentice-Hall, 1984.

Audition: Everything an Actor Needs to Get the Part. Michael Shurtleff. New York: Bantam, 1980.

Auditioning for the Musical Theatre. Fred Silver. New York: New Market, 1985.

Building a Character. Stanislavsky. New York: Theatre Arts, 1949.

Creating a Role. Stanislavsky. New York: Theatre Arts, 1961.

First Steps in Acting. Samuel Selden. New York: Appleton-Century-Crofts, 1947.

***Freeing the Natural Voice.* Kristin Linklater. New York: Drama Book Publishers, 1976.**

How to Audition. Gordon Hunt. New York: Harper and Row, 1979.

How to Audition for the Musical Theatre. Daniel Oliver. Drama Book, 1985.

Introduction to Acting. Stanley Kahan. Boston: Allyn and Bacon, 1962.

On the Art of the Stage. Stanislavsky. London: Faber and Faber, 1950.

***On the Technique of Acting.* Michael Chekhov. New York: HarperCollins, 1991.**

Papers on Acting. Branden Matthews, ed. New York: Hill and Wang, 1958.

Period Style for the Theatre. Douglas Russell. Boston: Allyn and Bacon, 1980.

Playing: An Introduction to Acting. Paul Kuritz. Englewood Cliffs, N.J.: Prentice-Hall, 1982.

***Respect for Acting.* Uta Hagen. New York: MacMillan, 1973.**

Roles in Interpretation. Judy Yordon. Dubuque: William Brown, 1982.

Strasberg's Method. S. Loraine Hull. Woodbridge: Ox Bow, 1985.

Techniques in Dramatic Art. Hallian Bosworth. New York: MacMillan, 1972.

Techniques of Acting. Ronald Hayman. New York: Holt, Rinehart, and Winston, 1969.

The Act and the Image. Rachmael ben Arram. New York: Odyssey, 1969.

The Act of Being. Charles Marowitz. New York: Taplinger, 1978.

The Actor at Work. Robert Benedetti. Englewood Cliffs, N.J.: Prentice-Hall, 1970.

The Actor's Eye. Morris Carnovsky. New York: Performing Arts Journal Publications, 1984.

The Actor's Ways and Means. Michael Redgrave. New York: Theatre Arts Books, 1953.

The Alexander Technique: The Revolutionary Way to Use Your Body for Total Energy. Sarah Barker. Toronto: Bantam Books, 1978.

The Art of Acting. John Dolman, Jr. New York: Harper, 1949.

The Complete Actor. Stanley Glenn. New York: Allyn and Bacon, 1977.

The Composite Art of Acting. Jerry Blunt. New York: MacMillan, 1966.

The Craftsman of Dionysus. Jerome Rockwood. Glenview: Scott, Foresman and Co., 1966.

The Dynamics of Acting. Joan Snyder. Skokie: National Textbook, 1972.

The Image of the Actor. Shearer West. New York: St. Martin's, 1991.

The Length and Depth of Acting. Edwin Duerr. New York: Holt, Rinehart, and Winston, 1962.

The Professional Actor: From Audition to Performance. Tom Markus. New York: Drama Book, 1980.

The Student Actor's Handbook: Theatre Games. Louis Dezseran. Palo Alto: Mayfield, 1975.

The Technique of Acting. Stella Adler. New York: Bantam, 1988.

The Total Actor. Raymond Rizzo. Indianapolis: Odyssey, 1975.

The Voice Book. Michael McCallion. New York: Theatre Arts Books, 1988.

Theatre Games. Clive Barker. London: Methuen, 1977.

Towards a Poor Theatre. Jerzy Grotowski. New York: Simon and Schuster, 1968.

Voice and Speech in the Theatre. Clifford Turner. New York: Sportshelf, 1982.

Technical Production

Supplies and services for all of your technical production needs that may not be available locally can be found in the essential resource **The New York Theatrical Sourcebook. Call or write Broadway Press, 120 Duane St., New York, NY 10007; (212) 693-0570.**

A History of Jewish Costumes. A. Rubens. London: Weidenfeld and Nicolson, 1967.

Costume Patterns and Design. Mike Tilke. London: A. Zwemmer, 1990. (If you choose only one book, this is it. Authentic costumes in color, showing variations in design.)

Costumes and Settings for Staging Historical Plays, Volume 1: The Classical Period. Jack Cassin-Scott. Boston: Plays, Inc., 1979.

Costumes of Greeks and Romans. Thomas Hope. New York: Dover, 1962.

Costuming a Play. Elizabeth B. Grimball and Rhea Wells. New York: The Century Company, 1925.

Costuming the Biblical Play. Lucy Barton. Boston: Walter H. Baker, 1937.

Create Your Own Stage Faces. Douglas Young. Englewood Cliffs, N.J.: Prentice-Hall, 1985.

Create Your Own Stage Lighting. Tim Streader and John A. Williams. Englewood Cliffs, N.J.: Prentice-Hall, 1985.

Historic Costume for the Amateur Theatre and How to Make It. Harold Melvill. Philadelphia: Dufour Editions, 1962.

Jesus of Nazareth. William Barclay. Cleveland: Collins and World, 1977 (Photographs from the Zeffirelli film; excellent for detail of Sadducees, Pharisees, and Roman soldiers).

Materials of the Scene: An Introduction to Technical Theatre. Welby B. Wolfe. New York: Harper and Row, 1977.

Patterns for Theatrical Costumes: Garments, Trims, and Accessories from Ancient Egypt to 1915. Katherine Strand Holkeboer. New York: Prentice Hall, 1984.

Scene Design and Stage Lighting. W. Oren Parker and Harvey K. Smith. New York: Holt, Rinehart, and Winston, 1985.

Stage Craft. Christ Hoggett. New York: St. Martin's Press, 1975.

Stage Makeup. 5th ed. Richard Corson. Englewood Cliffs, N.J.: Prentice Hall, 1975.

Stage Management. 3rd ed. Lawrence Stern. Boston: Allyn and Bacon, 1987.

The Art of Doing: Stage Makeup Techniques. Martin Jans. Amsterdam: van Dobbenburgh, 1986.

The Costume Designer's Handbook. Rosemary Ingham and Lis Cozey. New York: Prentice-Hall, 1983.

The Face Is A Canvas: The Design and Technique of Theatrical Makeup. Irene Corey. New Orleans: Anchorage Press, 1990.

The Stage Lighting Handbook, 3rd ed. Francis Reid. New York: Theatre Arts Books/Methuen, 1987.

The Theatre Props Handbook: A Comprehensive Guide to Theatre Properties, Materials, and Construction. Thurston James. White Hall, Va.: Betterway Publications, Inc., 1987.

Theatrical Makeup. Bert Broe. London: Pelham Books, 1984.

Drama in the Church

Addicted to Mediocrity. Franky Schaeffer. Westchester: Crossway Books, 1981.

Art and the Bible. Francis A. Schaeffer. Downers Grove, Ill.: InterVarsity Press, 1973.

Art in Action. Nicholas Wolterstorff. Grand Rapids: Eerdmans, 1980.

Art Needs No Justification. H. R. Rookmaaker. Downers Grove, Ill.: InterVarsity Press, 1978.

Christianity and the Theatre. Murray Watts. Edinburgh: Handsel Press, 1986.

Conscience on Stage. Harold Ehrenspenger. New York: Abingdon-Cokesbury Press, 1947.

Create a Drama Ministry. Paul M. Miller and Dan Dunlop. Kansas City: Lillenas Publishing Co., 1985.

Culture in Christian Perspective. Leland Ryken. Portland, Oreg.: Multnomah, 1987.

Developing a Drama Group. Robert Smyth, ed. Minneapolis: World Wide, 1989.

Imagination: Embracing a Theology of Wonder. Cheryl Forbes. Portland, Oreg.: Multnomah Press, 1986.

Religious Drama: Ends and Means. Harold Ehrenspenger. New York: Abingdon Press, 1962.

The Christian, the Arts, and Truth. Frank Gaebelein. Portland, Oreg.: Multnomah, 1987.

The Man Born to Be King. Dorothy L. Sayers. Grand Rapids: Eerdmans, 1943.

What to Do with the Second Shepherd on the Left. Deborah Craig-Claar. Kansas City: Lillenas Publishing Co., 1992.